Praise for *The Guide to Publishing Audiobooks* and author Jessica Kaye

"Want your voice to be heard? Then start by reading (or listening to) this book. Jessica Kaye's 6 Rules of Audiobook Publishing will make your recordings sound better and reach more listeners."
—Matthew Rubery, author of *The Untold Story of the Talking Book.*

"Jessica Kaye is the best of the best. She was with me syllable for syllable as I read my memoir—she laughed when I did, got choked up when we couldn't help it, and told me how to pronounce words I'd been saying in my head wrong all these years. Recording with Jessica will always be one of the high points of my career as an author. I'm first in line at her studio, hoping to record my next book!" —Hope Jahren, author of *Lab Girl*

"Thorough! Exhaustive! Accessible! As I read *The Guide to Publishing Audiobooks*, these three descriptions came to mind from beginning until end. Far more inclusive than a guide, Kaye has, quite simply, produced the audio publisher's bible. Pen in one hand, bonhomie in the other, she has managed to tell us everything we must know about what it takes to succeed as an audiobook publisher." —Paul Alan Ruben, writer, two-time Grammy-winning audiobook producer, director, and storytelling teacher

"Start your audiobook journey off right and increase your chances of success in the market with industry veteran Jessica Kaye's comprehensive guide!" —Michele Cobb, Executive Director, Audio Publishers Association, and publisher of *AudioFile Magazine* and MMB Media

D1470287

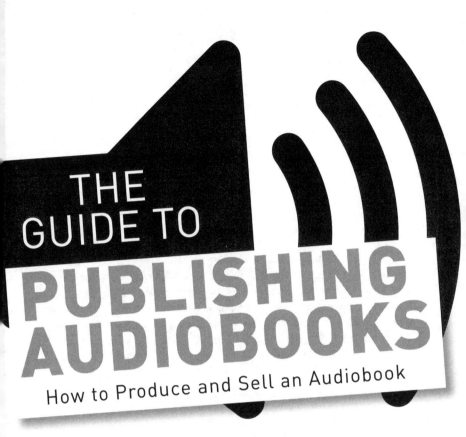

THE GUIDE TO
PUBLISHING AUDIOBOOKS

How to Produce and Sell an Audiobook

JESSICA KAYE

FROM THE MULTIPLE GRAMMY AWARD-WINNING
AUDIOBOOK DIRECTOR & PRODUCER

**WRITER'S
DIGEST
BOOKS**

WritersDigest.com
Cincinnati, Ohio

For more resources for writers, visit www.writersdigest.com.

23 22 21 20 19   5 4 3 2 1

Distributed in the U.K. and Europe by F+W Media International
Pynes Hill Court, Pynes Hill, Rydon Lane
Exeter, EX2 5SP, United Kingdom
Tel: (+44) 1392-797680, Fax: (+44) 1626-323319
E-mail: postmaster@davidandcharles.co.uk

Library of Congress Cataloging-in-Publication Data

ISBN-13: 978-1-4403-5433-5

Edited by Cris Freese and Amy Jones
Cover Designed by Jason Williams
Interior Designed by Liz Harasymczuk
Production Managed by Debbie Thomas

DEDICATION

To the memory of my parents, Joseph Mitchell Kaye and Miriam Diana Kaye, who infused our home with books and recordings and who, like me, never imagined a career could be made by combining those two things.

ACKNOWLEDGMENTS

I have been working with audiobooks since the 1980s, first through a class at UCLA in record production and in various ways ever since. I have been house counsel, publisher, distributor, outside counsel, producer, director, writer, and even narrator. That makes for a lot of relationships along the way and a lot of thanks to give.

First, I'd like to thank Cris Freese, formerly of F+W Media and Writer's Digest Books, for encouraging me to send the proposal that resulted in this book, and for his keen editorial notes. Heartfelt appreciation to Amy Jones, my editor at F+W Media and Writer's Digest Books, for her intelligent and incisive comments and her kind nature. Thanks to Kim Catanzarite for meticulously parsing my words and making this book better by her edits. Hats off to Jess Zafarris, Content Strategist at F+W Media and Writer's Digest Books, for her ability to think of smart ways to promote this project.

To Charles (Chuck) and Sally Anne Rosenberg, whose treasured friendship and willingness to travel in the name of writing and adventure are unmatched.

To the many people who contributed their time and expertise: Richard Brewer, Denise Buzy-Pucheu, Cassandra Campbell, John Cheary, Michele Cobb, Karen Commins, Carlin Craig, Frank Eakin, Kelly Gildea, George Hodgkins, Eileen Hutton, Jeffrey Kafer, Jorjeana Marie, Dan Musselman, Rochelle O'Gorman, and Matthew Rubery. If I have left anyone out, please accept my apologies and my gratitude.

To my writers group, as it currently is and as it has been over the past few years: to Richard James Brewer, Cassandra Campbell, Em Eldridge, Arthur Insana, Gabyinka Juglar, Dylan Landis, Maxine Nunes, and, wishfully, Julia Bricklin.

My gratitude to the late Zig Ziglar's team, especially Laurie Magers, and to Joe Sabah who each promptly and kindly granted permission to use the quote in the epigraph.

To Beth Faber Jacobs and Ken Jacobs, because I told you I'd add your names!

To the love and support of my incredible siblings and their incredible spouses. There's room to name them all, isn't there? Janet Kaye and Dan Kushel, Judith Lentini and John Lentini, Joel Kaye and Kimberly McKeever-Kaye, Jeremy Kaye and Lucille Kaye, Jocelyn Kaye and Andy Comendul, Jevera Hennessey and Bill Hennessey, Justine Kaye and Ronald King, and Johanna Greenfield and Jeffrey Greenfield.

Thanks to Kevin Mills, who was there for the founding of The Publishing Mills, the Grammy Award–winning audiobook publishing company which was named for our kids. His support, financial and emotional, made that venture, a major step in this career, possible.

My love and appreciation for Barbara Mills and the late Steve Mills, my wonderful parents-in-law.

There is nothing I do that doesn't include thoughts of my precious daughters, Clare Mills and Bryce Mills.

And to my sweet sweetheart, Richard Brewer, who has unwavering faith in everything I do. I hope I do the same for you, Richard.

To the evolution of the publishing industry, which keeps me awake and on my toes.

Lastly, to audiobook listeners the world over. Thanks to you, the quality of our work has gotten better and better. I don't know if the sky is the limit, but if there is a limit, let's keep striving to reach it.

ABOUT THE AUTHOR

Jessica Kaye lives in Los Angeles, California, where she began her career in publishing in 1986 as Vice President of Business Affairs for an entertainment company. There she worked on both television and feature film projects as well as publishing contracts.

In 1990, she founded The Publishing Mills, an audio publishing company that published approximately 200 titles. There, she produced two Grammy Award-nominated works, the Grammy Award-winning Best Comedy Recording, *Crank Calls* by Jonathan Winters and *The Chieftains*, an authorized biography of the famed Irish musical group.

Since her return to the practice of law in 2002, Jessica continues to produce audiobook recordings, having recorded hundreds of books for major publishers as well as independent publishers.

She has served as President of the Audio Publishers Association, where she currently serves as a member of the board and was a member of the Board of Governors for the Los Angeles Chapter of the Recording Academy. She founded Big Happy Family, LLC, www.bighappyfamilyaudio.com, a digital distribution company for audio programming. She serves on the board of the Scream Film Festival and has served on the board of the Victory Theatre Center in Burbank, California. Jessica was the creator and editor of, and a contributor to, the short story anthology *Meeting Across the River* (Bloomsbury, 2005), based on the Bruce Springsteen song of the same name. She has written for the anthologies *Occupied Earth* and *Culprits*.

Ms. Kaye is admitted to the practice of law in both California and Connecticut and is a partner at Kaye & Mills in Beverly Hills, California, www.kayemills.com.

TABLE OF CONTENTS

You don't have to be great to start, but you have to start to be great.

—ZIG ZIGLAR, QUOTING HIS FRIEND AND FELLOW MOTIVATIONAL SPEAKER JOE SABAH

Why This Guidebook?

Hi, I'm Jessica Kaye and I will be your tour guide through the landscape of audiobooks. My audiobook credentials are several decades long, from my introduction to the medium in a UCLA Extension class on record production in the 1980s, in which Nick Venet, the enthusiastic music record producer who taught the class, told the students that spoken word was the coming thing; to my work as an in-house attorney for an entertainment company that produced films, television mini-series, and audiobooks; to my own audiobook publishing company, The Publishing Mills, which received two Grammy nominations, including one win; to my current work as an attorney for numerous people in the audiobook industry and my continuing presence in the industry as a producer and director, resulting in more Grammy nominations and wins. In addition, I founded and own an audiobook distribution company, Big Happy Family, LLC, which provides audiobooks to digital retailers and libraries. This is not a humble autobiography but it does provide my bona fides, so that you can rest assured you are going to learn a lot from this book.

In the coming chapters, you will absorb information about how to determine whether any particular book is suitable for publishing in audio; a little about the history of the industry; how to acquire audio rights; how to decipher contracts; how to buy and sell rights if you control them; the keys to a quality-sounding audiobook; the nuts and bolts of making audiobooks; what to know about distribution, and a few legal matters impacting your publishing program. I will also confide my Six Rules of Audiobook Publishing.

There *is* a lot to learn, but please don't let it faze you. Once you have been working with audiobooks for a while, much of it will become almost instinctive, just as does any skill set you acquire. You will find your own way of doing things, some of which may be different from how I do things. That's part of what gives different publishers their different company personalities.

That will come in time. For now, whether you are a self-published author wanting to get your book in front of more prospective fans, a narrator interested in becoming a publisher, or an independent publisher contemplating developing or growing an audiobook line, this guide will serve as your starter manual in this flourishing area of publishing, and it can continue to be a reference book for you to reread as you come up against new circumstances over the course of your new—or renewed—career in publishing audiobooks.

CHAPTER 1

Why Produce Audiobooks?

At the time of this book's original publication in 2019, every year for the past six years, audiobook sales have been on an upward trajectory. They continue to be a bright spot in publishing, even as other areas slow down. The 2017 sales survey results released by the Audio Publishers Association, or APA, of which you will hear more later in the book, showed a 22.7 percent increase in audiobook revenue over the previous year, with an increase of 21.5 percent in units sold.

Audiobooks have made such an impact in their visibility that The British Library in London had an exhibit titled "Listen: 140 Years of Recorded Sound" that ran from October 6, 2017, through May 13, 2018. It was not about the spoken word alone, but that was a part of it.

So here you are, at the cusp of rising sales and increased publicity for the very thing you were thinking would be a smart addition to your business. Luck is what happens when preparation meets opportunity, according to some interpretations of the words of the ancient Roman Seneca. Echoing those thoughts centuries later, Branch Rickey has been oft quoted as saying, "Luck is the residue of hard work and design." Being in the right place at the right time is a more prosaic way of saying something similar. Those words apply to you, today.

WHY MORE AND MORE TRADITIONAL PUBLISHERS LOVE AUDIO

The major publishing houses have been including audiobooks in their publishing programs for decades. The market has grown from the days of fighting for acceptance and shelf space in bookstores in the 1980s to being an economic bright spot in the industry today. As sales and awareness of audiobooks grow, many of the non-major (by which I mean revenue, not quality of books) traditional publishers (by which I mean publishers who read and edit and publish books in the old-fashioned way, typically by offering an advance against a royalty or, if no advance, a royalty from *dollar one*, i.e. from the first revenue received) have begun either producing audiobooks or licensing the audio rights they hold to third parties. The difference between these two choices is significant, but both can bring revenue and value to the publisher's catalog. Producing audiobooks for sale still carries many of the same risks as publishing books because of the attendant costs of production, whereas licensing audio rights to third parties brings in revenue without any corresponding hard costs.

If you work within a traditional publishing house, it is time to consider audio rights as a valuable *subsidiary right*. *Subsidiary rights* are explained in detail in Chapter 4. For now, know that the phrase means rights other than the primary rights which, in this case, are rights that derive from the initial book contract.

If you are selling audio rights, your buyer will typically, but not always, be an independent audio publisher. This is primarily because the major publishers want to exploit audio rights to likely bestsellers or near bestsellers, and they have a great many of those types of books in their own stable. If the rights you are offering are connected to something which has exceptional marketability, such as a tie-in to a major motion picture, you may be able to strike a deal with one of the majors.

I have mixed feelings about publishers who do not produce audiobooks but ask for audio rights in their publishing agreements in order to resell them to audiobook publishers such as Blackstone Audio, Inc. and Tantor Media. Yes, being able to sell off those rights helps to subsidize the publishing of books and also can be seen as value added by making the author's books available in another format, but it also may give more revenue to the book publisher than is warranted. If you are a publisher doing this, I suggest you offer your authors a 60/40 split, rather than a standard split of 50/50, to recognize that the audiobook deal is thanks to your efforts and connections, but also to recognize that this type of sale may take relatively little effort on your part, especially if you have begun licensing your company's audio rights regularly to one or more audio publishers.

Whether you plan to be hands-on in producing and directing, or to hire one of the many freelance audiobook producers and directors to create the audiobooks for you, or you hire an in-house team, or you simply acquire audio rights when acquiring print rights and, in turn, sell those rights to audiobook publishing houses, audio rights are assets that demand attention. You can boost your bottom line and add the new format to your library of titles, or dispense with that and license the rights to third parties. As with all the different aspects of your publishing program, if you find the right audience, you can add *ka-ching* to your bottom line.

FOR NONTRADITIONAL PUBLISHERS AND INDIVIDUALS

The burgeoning of digital recording and distribution, and the consequent diminution in cost of production have allowed authors to transition to self-publishers without the stigma that self-publishing carried in past years. The companies that catered to self-published authors used to be called vanity presses—a pejorative term, at least in the eyes of those in the publishing business. These companies offered authors the ability to see their books in print, but with the catch that it was the author who paid for that metamorphosis from manuscript to bound book, unlike with traditional publishers. Often vanity presses were for works that were not well written, not well edited, and would not have been produced without the services of the vanity press. At other times, they were used for books the authors intended for a specific and limited audience, such as family members. In the past, as today, there were good books that never found a home with a legitimate publisher, just as there are countless talented musicians who never find a record label willing to produce and sell their music. Vanity presses allowed these authors to at least have copies of their books printed.[1] By and large, however, to be self-published was formerly a means of last resort.

That is no longer the case.

A number of authors are turning to self-publishing for various reasons including having the revenue from book sales come directly to them, being able to choose the cover, the timing of publication, and the formats—e-book, hardcover, paperback, audiobook, enhanced e-book. There are also many writers who choose to self-publish because they tried their luck with agents or traditional publishers without the desired results. Some of you who have picked up this guide have already been published by a third-party publisher and now are thinking of doing it yourself. Some of you have already published books on your own and want to branch into audiobook publishing. Some of you have already published or

---

1 Legitimate publishers do not ask the author to pay to be published. If you have an offer for your manuscript which includes a demand for monies from you, that is not a contract you should sign. It is perfectly legitimate for you to pay to have your book printed, but be aware that makes *you* the publisher. This is the modern version of a vanity press. This differs from audiobook publishing, however, where you may very well need to pay to have your book transformed into an audiobook.

produced audiobooks and want to get better at it and do more of it. No matter the reason you are considering publishing an audiobook, your goal should be to make it a *good* audiobook. If you don't want that, why do it at all?

And that's why this book exists: to serve as your guide to publishing a *good* audiobook. After all, your reputation and your sales depend on the quality of your work.

Now let's get you started.

CHAPTER 2

Audiobook Industry Overview

In Chapter 1, we touched on the growth of audiobook publishing as a result of digital solutions for both recording and distribution. Well, just as digital tools made it easier to produce audiobooks, they also made it easier for consumers to access them. The confluence of the increase in numbers of digital audiobooks being published along with the near ubiquity of electronic devices such as phones, laptops, and tablets, and the decrease in the price of audiobooks because they no longer required manufacturing, packaging, and shipping, have combined to propel sales upward.

Libraries began adding digital audiobooks to their offerings and retail download sites proliferated. People were listening to audiobooks in the car, at home, on the move because the audiobooks were on their hard drive, mp3 device, or accessed via an app on their phones! All of this tremendous growth in portability without diminution of quality has built the juggernaut that is the audiobook industry.

A BRIEF HISTORY OF AUDIOBOOKS

Spoken word storytelling likely has been around for almost as long as humans have been able to speak. It predated writing and printing. Perhaps some of your earliest memories are of someone telling you a story.

Despite its early origins, for many years the idea of the spoken word as a replacement or even a complement to the printed word was a little shocking, at least to the bookselling community. For years, when anyone asked what I did for a living, my answer usually brought two responses: "What is that?" or "Oh, you mean for the blind?"

In *The Untold Story of the Talking Book*, author Matthew Rubery made this observation about the origins of the audiobook:

> Yet it is equally important to note that recorded books were never meant for people with disabilities alone. It is a misconception that recorded books began as a format for blind readers before being taken up by a broader readership in the second half of the twentieth century in the form of audiobooks. From the outset the audience for recorded speech reached well beyond those with disabilities. Edison's hypothetical audience included "the average reader" lacking either the time or the inclination to hold a book. His statement is one of the first to characterize reading as a secondary activity intended to accompany other pursuits. More important, it endorsed the professionalization of reading by insisting on the increased "amusement," "enjoyment," and "profit" to be had from listening to a trained reader. There is no idealization here of the silent reader's ability to voice texts for himself or herself. Even if audiences were already reading, Edison implies, they were not reading very well.

Generally speaking, the current audiobook industry has its roots in the 1980s, when bookstores such as Waldenbooks and Barnes & Noble somewhat grudgingly gave shelf space to the format. Denise Buzy-Pucheu was the audiobook buyer for Waldenbooks in the late 1980s, and she confirms that the chain was unwilling to dedicate much shelf space to audiobooks and was especially unwilling to give much unabridged audio a chance because the price point was high.

"Unabridged was considered more for the library and institutional markets because of price point," she said. Back then, she added, "It was a combination of shelf space [and] trying to get the consumer to purchase the medium, since most audiobook customers were those driving long distances in cars. No one was advertising audiobooks, even in holiday catalogs. Subliminal audio did well at certain times of the year, notably during the first quarter, when people made New Year's resolutions. Old-time radio (OTR) did well at Christmas. [As f]or general audiobooks, mysteries and audiobooks based on bestsellers did best."

Those of you who remember those days and listened to audiobooks back then might have preferred or abhorred abridgments and, either way, wondered why they existed. They existed in large part because, other than for short books, an unabridged production would have taken up more shelf space than bookstores were willing to allocate to this nascent format. The recordings were on cassette tapes then, and that required large packages, which were bulky and heavy and expensive. They were expensive because both the packaging and the cassettes themselves were costly to produce. The stores wanted to put more tried-and-true items out for sale; audiobooks were risky business.

It was primarily due to the bulk and necessarily high price of long recordings that abridgements were the dominant format for a number of years. That satisfied the buyers at the chains who could take risks on less-expensive programs that took up nominal amounts of space. Shelves with abridged audiobooks and a few specialty unabridged recordings began to appear in audiobook departments in bookstores in the 1980s.

That's a little bit of backstory to explain the landscape of commercial audiobooks. For a detailed look at the history of the recorded spoken word, I recommend *The Untold Story of the Talking Book* by Matthew Rubery (Harvard University Press, 2016).

BOOK TRADE DISCOUNT RATES

When you sell an audiobook, or any type of book, to a retailer in the book trade, they receive a discount off the retail price. They have to get a discount because if they paid full retail price, they would not make any money when they sold the item to a customer. There are exceptions but for the most part, publishing industry discounts fall between 30 to 60 percent. When you get to the high end of the discount rates, more than 55 percent, you are either selling to someone who has superior bargaining power—a megastore, for example—or you are making what is known as a nonreturnable sale. Nonreturnable sales are just what they sound like: The customer is buying audiobooks that they are not allowed to return. This is a rare bright spot in the publisher's world: a sale that remains a sale. You give the customer a large discount, and they waive their right to return products.

If you are already a publisher then you know that book publishing is, for the most part, a *returnable* business. If this is new language to you, returnable sales mean that anything you have sold to a bookstore may be returned at any time, and you must credit the customer's account or even cut them a check. This can happen surprisingly soon after shipping the product to the retailer, or it can be months or even years later. For many small publishers, receiving returns makes the difference between being in the black, when you believe you are expecting payment of outstanding invoices to, instead, being in the red because of returns. *Returns* are the bane of the publishing industry, but it has long been this way, and although a few publishers take a stand against it now and again, it is still how things work. A clothing store may mark down a blouse that did not sell at full price but a bookstore can simply box up items that haven't sold and return them.

Obviously, many bookstores do have items marked with low sale prices. This is rarely because they have marked down a book in the same way the fashion industry or other retailers might mark down the goods they sell. When booksellers have sales on books, it's typically because they have discounted best-selling books in order to compete with Amazon.com, barnesandnoble.com, and other online booksellers, or the store has purchased *overstocks* or *remaindered* books. As a publisher, you should understand the difference between these two terms.

Publishers have *overstocks* when their inventory on any particular title or titles far exceeds what is needed to fulfill orders in the foreseeable future. This could be as a result of overprinting, or it could be due to returns. For example, a publisher may have printed 10,000 copies of a book, anticipating that they will receive initial orders for 8,000 units, and wanting to have enough copies on hand to fill new orders or reorders. It may be that they don't have many reorders or new orders and so they have many books in inventory that appear to be unneeded. The publisher can choose to deeply discount the price of the overstock books and sell them off, simply to recoup their manufacturing monies and to avoid having books taking up space in a warehouse. Unless the publisher owns their own warehouse, they are likely paying monthly rental fees for the space in which they store their books. It is often economically more sensible to get rid of the extra books at a low price than to keep them on hand, hoping for a future buyer. Overstocks are not necessarily the end of the book's lifespan, but just a temporary housecleaning measure.

Remainders are similar in that they are sold to retailers at a deeply discounted price. Remainders are typically the books in inventory at the end of their publishing life. It could be that the contract for the book has expired; it could be that the sales of the title are low enough that the publisher is taking it out of print.

When the publisher removes it from print, they need to do something with the inventory because they are either losing the right to sell the book or permanently clearing out a title that is no longer selling very well. In both cases, cutting the price deeply in order to get the product out of the warehouse, rather than not sell it at all, makes sense.

If you have ever bought books at a low price and seen a pen mark along the bottom, the side, or the top of the book, that book was remaindered or sold as overstock. That pen marking is one way publishers ensure that books sold for very little are not returned by someone claiming to have paid the wholesale or full retail price.

There are companies that specialize in purchasing large or small lots of books and audiobooks and, in turn, reselling them to retailers. Working with these overstock and remainder buyers is a common way to handle getting rid of excess inventory. These days, both overstocks and remainders are less relevant than in even the recent past, due to the diminution of the number of hard copy products. If you do have hard copy units to get rid of, selling them at low prices can bring back capital to help you with the costs of newer projects.

Returns were and still are a concern for publishers, but back to our story of how this industry evolved in the 1980s and 1990s, eventually audiobooks started *selling through*—which means that consumers did purchase them, i.e. they sold through to the end user, the customer. Those that did not sell through were still returned to the publisher, but the bookstore chains and, hence, the publishers, could see that audiobooks were working as a medium and deserving of shelf space at the store and of space in overall publishing programs.

Even in the early days, there were a few companies that were able to get unabridged products onto the shelves. Some had clever packaging that made the product stand out or fit in smaller spaces than standard packaging would allow, such as Great American Audio Corp. Others, such as Brilliance Corporation, created technological methods of having more audio in each package without needing more cassettes. Brilliance did this by using two channels on each cassette. Doing so made it feasible for unabridged audiobooks to gain a place on the shelves at pricing that was competitive with some of the abridgements. From the consumer standpoint, these were simple to use. They were put into a cassette player just like any other cassette but with instructions to turn the dial to one stereo channel at a time rather than hearing both, as is more usual, doubling the amount of listening time contained on each cassette. This enabled Brilliance to bring such unabridged books to market as Dean Koontz titles, including *Watchers* and *Midnight*; Tom Clancy books *Hunt for Red October* and *Clear and Present Danger*; Ken Follett's *Pillars of the Earth* and *Eye of the Needle*; and Jean M. Auel's Clan of the Cave Bear series.

In the late 1990s, CDs became the predominant format for audiobooks, at first slowly and then more rapidly displacing cassettes, as new cars came with CD players and cassette players were phased out. CDs are slim and many can fit into a package more easily and with less weight than cassettes. That was an advantage that allowed more and more unabridged productions to come to market. The technological disadvantage of CDs was that the maximum running time was about twenty minutes less than the maximum running time of a cassette. But what was lost in capacity was gained in accessibility. You could scan a CD to jump to a chapter easily, or jump back if you daydreamed during part of the story. You could go back to that track and voilà, the story picked up wherever you had tuned out. That was the case with cassettes as well, but rewinding a cassette, although not difficult, was a more time-consuming and manual way to find the place where you'd tuned out.

Digital streams and downloads came along toward the end of the 1990s and into the early twenty-first century. Many publishers approached the new format cautiously, with fear of piracy by those unscrupulous enough to take audiobooks without paying for them. Some of the major publishers indicated their disinclination to use the new format, but over time, as the download sites proved themselves, everyone realized the sales potential was greater than the downside.

Now you are up to speed on the evolution of the audiobook. What formats will come next is anyone's guess.

PIRACY

Evolution brings new worries.

It used to be that audiobook publishers joked that they wished their products were desirable enough to warrant worrying about piracy. That was a little flippant and tongue-in-cheek, but what was being expressed was the desire that audiobooks were high profile enough to make publishers concerned about protecting such a popular product from theft.

Digital streaming and downloading granted that wish. Today, audio publishers do worry about piracy, which has become a real problem. The impact on sales has not been measured, so far as I am aware, and overall the medium is healthy, but that doesn't mean piracy is harmless. It infringes rights and steals revenue from rightful owners. Piracy needs to be countered and combatted wherever and whenever possible. It is no less wrong than pickpocketing or shoplifting.

This conversation about infringing rights leads us to a short discussion about copyright and what it means. The United States Copyright Office (www.copyright.gov) defines copyright in the following manner.

A form of protection provided by the laws of the United States for "original works of authorship," including literary, dramatic, musical, architectural, cartographic, choreographic, pantomimic, pictorial, graphic, sculptural, and audiovisual creations. "Copyright" literally means the right to copy but has come to mean that body of exclusive rights granted by law to copyright owners for protection of their work. Copyright protection does not extend to any idea, procedure, process, system, title, principle, or discovery. Similarly, names, titles, short phrases, slogans, familiar symbols, mere variations of typographic ornamentation, lettering, coloring, and listings of contents or ingredients are not subject to copyright.

On a practical level, here is what you need to know: Copyright is automatically created at the same time a piece of intellectual property is created. As soon as ideas are committed to a permanent and fixed form, such as a recording of an audiobook, there is a copyright attached to it. It is also important to know that ideas themselves are not protectable by copyright. It is the *expression* of ideas that is protectable. That is what "committed to a permanent and fixed form" means: a piece of art, a piece of writing, a film, a sound recording.

That unregistered inherent copyright entitles you to a number of rights. Those rights, subject to some limitations spelled out in the federal law[1] include the right to do and to authorize the following, as set out in Title 17, Chapter 1, Section 106:

> Subject to sections 107 through 122, the owner of copyright under this title has the exclusive rights to do and to authorize any of the following:
>
> (1) to reproduce the copyrighted work in copies or phonorecords;

---

1 If you are so inclined, you can read about the specific exceptions to the rights granted to the owner of an unregistered copyright contained in Title 17 of the United States Code, Sections 107 through 122.

(2) to prepare <u>derivative works</u> based upon the copyrighted work;

(3) to distribute copies or <u>phonorecords</u> of the copyrighted work to the public by sale or other transfer of ownership, or by rental, lease, or lending;

(4) in the case of literary, musical, dramatic, and choreographic works, pantomimes, and motion pictures and other <u>audiovisual work</u>, to perform the copyrighted work publicly;

(5) in the case of literary, musical, dramatic, and choreographic works, pantomimes, and pictorial, graphic, or sculptural works, including the individual images of a motion picture or other audiovisual work, to <u>display</u> the copyrighted work publicly; and

(6) in the case of <u>sound recordings,</u> to perform the copyrighted work publicly by means of a digital audio transmission.

"So," you may be thinking, "If copyright automatically attaches to my audiobook recording, why do I need to bother to register a copyright with the U.S. Copyright Office? Isn't that an unnecessary expense and an unnecessary use of my time?"

The answer to those questions is that there are statutory remedies available to those who register their copyrights. The most protection is offered to those who register within three months of publication. There is still value to registering the copyright even after that three month window, however. Without registering the copyright with the U.S. Copyright Office, you cannot bring suit in federal court for copyright infringement. Without the *timely* filing of the registration, you are unable to obtain statutory damages for copyright infringement. If you do register your copyright with the U.S. Copyright Office, but later than three months after publication, you are able to bring suit for copyright infringement, but you will be limited to *actual damages*, and not entitled to statutory damages.

The U.S. Copyright Office has an FAQ titled, "Why should I register my work if copyright protection is automatic?" Their answer provides additional information. It reads:

> Registration is recommended for a number of reasons. Many choose to register their works because they wish to have the facts of their copyright on the public record and have a certificate of registration. Registered works may be eligible for statutory damages and attorney's fees in successful litigation. Finally, if registration occurs within five years of publication, it is considered *prima facie* evidence in a court of law.

Prima facie is a term meaning at first sight or on its face, and in a court of law, it means sufficient to prove a fact to the judge or jury, who will accept it as proof that what the evidence states is true unless rebutted with opposing evidence. That's just one of the ways a registered copyright can come in handy.

I know, that is a lot of legalese and probably sounds a lot like "Blah blah, Ginger, blah blah, Ginger" to most of you. (Fill in your own name in the place of Ginger.)[2]

Here is an example of what the legalese means: You produced and own an audiobook recording and you have learned that someone has been illegally selling copies of it. You sue them for infringing your copyright. You did not register your copyright within three months of the publication date, but you did register it later. During the lawsuit, the defendant admits he sold ten copies of your audiobook at ten dollars each. He grossed $100 dollars from infringing your copyright, and you are entitled to a judgment against him in the sum of $100.

In an alternate universe, you *did* register the copyright within three months of publication. Statutory damages may be $750 to $30,000, per incident of infringement. This doesn't mean for each

---

2 "Blah blah, Ginger" is a reference to an iconic Gary Larson cartoon. If you are unfamiliar with it, do an internet search for it. You can thank me later.

sale the pirate made, as these ten sales may be viewed by a court as a single incident of infringement. Even so, you can see that you are compensated better by being able to collect statutory damages than by collecting only actual damages. The registration may also entitle you to attorney's fees, meaning that the infringer will be ordered to reimburse you for your legal fees. This can be actual legal fees incurred or a different amount that the court deems reasonable. Without timely registration, you will be out of pocket for your legal representation.

You may be wondering why these are called statutory damages. It is because Congress passed a law giving the right to collect these damages for copyrights that are timely registered and so these rights come from a statute. Statute ... statutory.

Owning the copyright generally means ownership of the right to use the intellectual property as you choose, e.g. to sell it, rent it, license it to a third party, or to keep it out of the marketplace entirely. In a few paragraphs, we will get into an exception to the copyright holder's right to use the intellectual property.

The copyright owner is called the rightsholder. Anyone who does not have that grant of rights from the rightsholder or their licensee, and is purporting to sell or give away the audio, is infringing the copyright.

This does not refer to someone who bought a hard copy and then lends it to someone else to listen to. Just as you can lend someone a book, depending on the format you have obtained and where you obtained it, you can lend an audiobook. There is something called the First Sale Doctrine, which makes it permissible. The First Sale Doctrine is explained in more depth in Chapter 10.

But when you download an audiobook, you may want to take a look at the contract you signed when you joined the website from which you downloaded it to see whether you are allowed to share the audio files with anyone. Maybe you can. Maybe the number of times you can share it is limited and maybe it isn't. But it could be that you thought you purchased something outright, believing that you now own it, but instead you may have only purchased a license to listen to it, albeit perhaps multiple times.

What Happens to the Recording When the Contract Term Expires?

As an aside, there may be occasions when the copyright holder cannot, in fact, sell, rent, or license their intellectual property, most likely because of a contract restricting those rights. An example of this is an audiobook produced under a license with an expiration date. The publisher owns the copyright to the recording, but after the contract's expiration date, they no longer have the right to distribute it to the public, whether by gift, loan, or sale. If someone else subsequently licenses the audio rights, they may want to license your recording from you rather than start from scratch and record it anew. That would be a legal use of your recording and it has been known to happen, on occasion.

If you are the rightsholder and are licensing the rights to a third party rather than publishing the audiobook yourself, you can try to add a clause to the licensing agreement to provide that the licensee will transfer ownership of the copyright in the recording to you when their contract term expires. That way you will have your rights back, and you will also have a finished recording that you can use as you wish, to sell, rent, sublicense, or lock away in a vault, never to see the light of day again. Otherwise, once the license terminates, you have the rights back and can license them to someone else or decide to hold on to them, but you will have no rights to the recording the audio publisher made. They cannot do anything with it other than admire it or, as noted, license it to your new licensee, but neither can you do anything with it, unless you and they agree to a transfer of ownership or, of course, a renewal of their right to distribute the recording.

MORE ABOUT PIRACY

Now, back to the issue of piracy. It is those websites purporting to sell or give away audiobooks that have not been licensed to them that are a problem. These sites are popping up with increasing frequency, sometimes making publishers feel as though they are in a never-ending game of Whac-A-Mole®. How much they are draining from the coffers of publishers and authors I do not know, but I do know that it is no longer a joking matter to contemplate audiobook piracy.

If you spend a little time on YouTube, you can find a lot of audiobooks available for download. Some belong to the person or company who has uploaded it. Many do not. That is another form of piracy. The good news is that YouTube, a company owned by Alphabet, which is the parent company of Google, does pay attention to take-down notices. Take-down notices also are discussed in more detail in Chapter 10.

DRM

Do these threats of piracy mean most audiobooks sold digitally have *DRM*?

DRM is the acronym for *digital rights management*. This is used by other media, too, not just publishing. In our industry, its primary use has been to limit the devices upon which the audiobook can be heard. The intention is to prevent material from being shared illegally. There is no unified opinion on whether or not DRM combats piracy effectively. Nevertheless, it is a tool available to publishers who wish to use it.

Even so, fewer and fewer audiobooks have DRM protection. Consumers were unhappy about DRM, because it could prevent someone who legitimately purchased an audiobook from listening to it on the multiple devices they own. For example, they may have downloaded an audiobook onto their laptop and wanted to transfer it to their phone in order to continue listening in the car but have been unable to do so. This goes back to the threshold question: Do you own the audiobook or do you own a license to listen to it? If the latter, what restrictions does that license impose?

Many sites and publishers no longer use DRM, but it is not entirely a thing of the past. It is worth noting that DRM was not always successful. Just as hackers find ways to get into protected databases, so do pirates find ways to pirate presumably protected materials. I have always thought books which give instructions that can be followed by criminals to pursue illegal gain were irresponsible, so I will not disclose even some of the simplest methods of piracy. The growth of piracy speaks for itself.

Piracy Redux

Even though I have spent time introducing you to DRM, piracy, and copyright law, ultimately, I do not think you should include piracy in the equation of whether or not to publish audiobooks. I don't mean you should ignore the issue. Piracy of your program may or may not happen. If it does, try to shut it down. Hire an attorney or a rights alert company to keep an eye out for you or to send a *cease and desist letter* or follow *take-down procedures* if the pirated audiobooks are found on legitimate sites such as YouTube. For law-abiding sites that carry infringing materials, there are methods to deal with removing the infringing material. The other sites, the truly illegal sites, may or may not be cowed by the threat of legal action—that is, if you can even identify who is running the site and are able to contact them. Sometimes even that is a daunting task. As mentioned, I talk more about this in Chapter 10.

What I do mean is that piracy is real and may or may not become an issue you have to deal with, but it is not a big enough factor for you to include it in your cost/benefit assessment of whether to publish a particular title. It is something you should be aware of as the steward of intellectual property.

Before assuming your rights have been infringed, you must do your due diligence. I have had clients tell me that their audiobook was pirated or their rights infringed, but upon closer look, I have found the site was legitimate and had a proper license, if not directly from the client then a sublicense from someone to whom the client had, indeed, authorized to sell their recordings, including the right for that licensee to permit sales by third party sellers. Be sure, or at least be as sure as you possibly can be, before concluding that your work is in the hands of a pirate.

Consider another client, who believed his audiobooks were being pirated. When I found the URL he was concerned about, I saw that the site claimed to be giving away free downloads of his work. There was a link to click to get to the freebie.

I did not click the link to see whether it did lead to his audio files. It seemed to me more likely that clicking the link would infect my computer with a virus. I asked the client whether he had clicked the link and advised him not to do so, if he hadn't already, in case the virus theory was correct. He had not and agreed that was a prudent course of action. That may be one site where we never learn whether the publisher's audiobooks really were being given away for free or whether there was something else going on there.

The moral of that story is that even if you suspect piracy, suspect links even more. Hire someone to check out the suspected pirate if you can afford to do so. See if you can discuss it with others in the audiobook community to learn whether anyone has experience with that website. You may even chalk it up to the cost of doing business, akin to shrinkage in the hard copy retail market. Shrinkage means loss of products to theft.

The way this client found the pirated site was by using Google Alerts. I am not endorsing that as a means of monitoring the availability of your audiobooks. I am simply pointing out that it is one potential tool.

One more caveat: Do not immediately publicly claim that a specific site or person is pirating your audiobooks, because if you are incorrect, you may have defamed the person or business. Do your due diligence here, as well.

Check with others in the industry. There are listservs which are populated by audiobook publishers, narrators, and the like. See if anyone else is aware of the website that concerns you. Maybe someone else's experience will be helpful. Gauge that person's gravitas, though, before jumping on the bandwagon to decry a website as illegally disseminating audiobooks.

The resources section of this book includes the names of a few companies which can monitor and assist with piracy protection.

SUMMARY

You have had an introduction to some of the history, business practices, and legal issues pertinent to audio publishers. You've looked at the growth of the commercial audiobook industry in the 1980s and 1990s, and items such as discount rates, returns, overstocks, remainders, piracy, copyright registration, contract expiration, and DRM. That's the welcoming committee. There's more to come.

CHAPTER 3

Taking Audiobook Inventory—Is It Feasible to Turn Your Book into an Audiobook?

Assessing Your Book's Potential for Audio,

Including a Cost/Benefit Analysis with a

Typical Budget

Let's do a feasibility analysis. This means analyzing your assets to determine whether the sales of the audio will make the project economically worthwhile. For starters, think about the prospective audience for your book. Are you able to estimate its approximate size? Is it big enough to warrant producing the audiobook? Economics may not be the only reason to pursue a project, but they are an important element in analyzing feasibility.

HOW BIG ARE YOUR PLANS?

Are you considering publishing just one audiobook or are you thinking of working with multiple books? An important consideration in just about any publishing business is that a library of titles, a bulk of works, is typically necessary to provide a significant income stream. If you are hoping to become an audio publisher of meaningful size, then by definition you need to have a number of titles to turn into audiobooks.

But maybe you are filling a niche or just want to publish a specific audiobook or a few of them. Some of you will have just one audiobook you want to create. That's okay, of course. A one-title audiobook venture is more likely to be a labor of love than a building block toward a full catalog of audiobooks. Whether a single title or many, you will want to run an analysis for each. The beginning process is the same, regardless of the number of titles you plan to produce.

If you are seeking to make a profit, you need to look at clues as to whether your project is likely to earn decent revenue. For instance, if you are licensing a book that hasn't come out yet, you'll want to see if you can glean the size of the first print run the publisher is planning for the book and what kind of marketing plans they have. Is it going to have a large first printing? How large is large? Is there going to be advertising? Are they underwriting a book tour? Are they doing a virtual book tour? Are they doing nothing? Is the book the basis of an upcoming major motion picture? Or is it the basis of a motion picture that will come and go? And if it comes and goes, is it going to be in the public eye long enough to make audiobook buyers aware of the film and hence the audiobook, or is it not? Try to be objective in your analysis.

Of course, you cannot know the answers to all of these questions because some things strike a chord with the public unexpectedly, and some things seemingly predestined for greatness fall flat.

A good example of smart audiobook publishing took place a year or so before the film *12 Years a Slave* was released. Frank Eakin of Eakin Film & Publishing contacted me back then to say that his company was planning to publish an audiobook based on the actual journal written by the gentleman that the film was about.

This was very smart of them, because the book had long been in the public domain. They cast Louis Gossett Jr. to narrate it.

The film did beautifully, as you probably know, garnering both box office success and Academy Awards. We cannot know how well the audiobook would have done in the absence of the film's success, but certainly because the film was so successful and provided a lot of publicity on which the audiobook could piggyback, it likely did much better than it would have if somebody had just said, "This is a really interesting journal. I think I'll publish this as an audiobook." If there was nothing to go along with it, no other form of publicity, odds are they would have sold a few copies here and there, but it wouldn't have made its way to a significant number of people's awareness. All in all, *12 Years a Slave* is an exemplar of the kind of project that is attuned to events likely to garner publicity, to allow an audiobook to benefit from the success of an aligned project. It is an example of the sort of tom-toms you can listen for in order to make an educated guess about whether a particular project makes economic sense.

This was the very first audiobook published by Eakin Film & Publishing. The backstory to this is amazing and wonderful. Frank's mother found a copy of Solomon Northrup's journal when she was a child, and she remained fascinated by it her entire life. This fascination turned into a master's thesis on the journal, and later she published a modern edition of it. She worked to preserve a building on the plantation where Northrup had been a slave and did a great deal of research over the decades. When she passed away in 2009, her children became the guardians of her work. This was a very unusual circumstance indeed but how fortunate that Frank Eakin had the awareness and reverence for his mother's work to think to bring *12 Years a Slave* to life as an audiobook.

You might not have a close relative with a passion that turns into a hit film, but many of us have ears attuned to things that find a place in the public's interest. It may be that nothing has particularly caught your imagination but you can still hone the ability to pay attention to events both cultural and societal.

Films are not the only kind of tie-in publicity upon which audio publishers can depend. There are news events, some of which are predictable and some of which are not. Predictable ones include election cycles, long-term social issues, major sports events, and perennial holidays such as Christmas, to name a few.

You may be able to capitalize on an unexpected newsworthy moment if your company is nimble and able to quickly find material, cast it, record it, edit it, and get it into the distribution stream. This could be anything from an unexpected bursting onto the scene of a social issue or a sudden interest that captivates millions due to Mother Nature (such as an upcoming and well-publicized meteor shower). It can be anything with a high profile.

One of the yardsticks I mentioned as a piece of the equation in gauging potential success is the size of a book's initial print run. In the olden days, not so very long ago, when publishers almost always produced hard copy versions of audiobooks, meaning a physical copy such as a CD or cassette, the loose rule of thumb was that audiobooks would sell about 10 percent of what the book sales were. Thus, if you know that a publisher is going to do a print run of 100,000, you can guesstimate that you might sell 10,000 audiobooks. That's not a bad sales figure for an audiobook. If you learn the print publisher is going to print just 2,000 copies, you might want to think again about whether it is worth it to you to try to put out an audiobook that might sell 200 copies. It may not even sell 200 copies. Now, you still may have reasons to do it, and there may be ways to bring it to people's attention. But this sort of math is one thing that can help you decide whether or not it is worthwhile to publish any particular audiobook.

If you are licensing the rights to a book that has already been published, then to use this measuring stick, you will need to know what the book sales have been. There are some tools on the market for that, but absent those tools, try this one: Ask the publisher. They should be able to give you rough figures because they should understand that such information helps you decide what to offer for the audio rights. That said, a publisher may not wish to share this information and, especially if you are unknown to them, may not provide it.

Other ways of discerning book sales include subscribing to NPD DecisionKey (formerly BookScan), which uses *point of sale* data collection for hard copy book sales. This is not a free service. If you are already a publisher, perhaps you have a subscription to it to obtain your publications' point of sales data. DecisionKey doesn't collect data from all stores—not even all bookstores—but it does collect and collate data from a number of retailers. The sales number you get for any particular title may require some extrapolation to get to the big picture, but it can at least provide a starting point for your analysis.

Another company, Prague-based BookCore, is working on an algorithm to aid in providing assumptions about sales of specific titles. BookCore already provides aggregating sales data from several key sites including Amazon, Google Play, Apple iBooks, and Smashwords for publishers to track their e-book sales. The working title of their nascent analytical program for approximating books sold by other publishers is BookCore Market Analytics. Keep your eyes open for it, if you are in need of this kind of tool to decide whether to acquire audio rights to a book already in the marketplace.

If you decide that this project is worth it to you economically, then you next need to determine whether it is actually capable of making the transition to audio. In fact, you could flip these first two criteria because both topics are essential to your success: the suitability for audio and an approximation of likely sales figures.

For suitability, start with a basic examination of the material you want to turn into an audiobook. Is the project fiction or non-fiction? Is it mainstream prose, or is it a textbook that uses charts and graphs or photographs? Is it a book with an unusual layout, such as with words printed in the margins or perhaps in concentric circles? Perhaps it presents other challenges in converting the written word to audio. All of these types of books have been translated into audio. Some are more difficult than others to shepherd to a successful transition, but with elbow grease and determination, it usually can be done.

For the analysis of your project, genre is less relevant than style. Both a romance novel and *War and Peace* are equally translatable to audio with relative ease because the narrative follows typical prose patterns. There is nothing tricky about the content or the manner in which it has been expressed. This doesn't include the need to be able to pronounce any French or Russian words in the English translation of Tolstoy, much less if you choose to publish it in the original Russian—that certainly could be challenging. No, this is just to say that the linguistic structure of each of these is made up of straightforward sentences that move the story forward in standard ways.

Many books with graphs or charts can also successfully transition into audio, but they may require some adapting, which is usually done by the audio producer or director, not the author. Contact with the author is often desirable, to help parse the text when needed or to provide pronunciations, if the director cannot find them and the author happens to have them. A good example of this is a nonfiction book that details places and persons whom the author has interviewed but whose names are not popping up in the director's preparation prior to recording. For graphs and charts, if the information is already described in the text and the pictures are strictly illustrative, then no rewriting is necessary, except, perhaps, to eliminate references to those visual aids.

Imagine a pie chart showing the types of movies teenagers aged thirteen to sixteen say are their favorites. Your text will consist of something like this: "As you can see by the pie chart in Figure A, 20 percent of teens like comedies best, 30 percent prefer mysteries, and 50 percent like foreign films best." You can tell this is a made-up example because the pie chart doesn't include horror films, and the scale is tilted too heavily toward foreign films! Whether the pie chart is accurate or not, one way to adapt it to audio is to delete the opening phrase, "As you can see by the pie chart in Figure A," and begin the sentence with, "20 percent of teens like comedies best." Similarly, a graph that shows the rise of the use of automobiles in the twentieth century in each decade could be paraphrased. You get the idea.

Sometimes the graphs or charts are more integral than in those examples, and that makes them a bit harder to adapt for audio. You may have pages of data provided to the reader in lieu of text— that requires the task of translating the data into words that fit the audiobook in tone and content. If you are not the author, you may need to obtain the author's consent or advice in order to translate that part of the book into words that will work for the audiobook. No matter what, you need to ensure that your translation of a pictorial representation into language accurately states the information being provided. If the subject matter requires expertise, you may not be in a position to know whether the transition from graph to words is accurate. This is another test of whether the book can successfully transition to audio.

Often an audiobook will make reference to a PDF that the listener can find on a website or download. When the publisher decides there is enough text to narrate an audiobook but also significant enough visual content that should be made available to the customer, the PDF is a useful tool for your audiobook tool kit. The URL for the PDF can be mentioned in the audiobook recording. As the narrator comes upon graphs or other things the listener will be able to see on the website or via downloading the PDF, he can say something such as, "On the accompanying PDF, which you will find at www.bestaudiobookeverPDF .com ..." As other items available on the PDF come up in the recording, it will not be necessary to give the URL each time; the narrator can simply say, "... in a graph you can see in the accompanying PDF," or a variation on that theme.

A KEY ELEMENT

How important is the choice of narrator? This is not a rhetorical question. Can you think of an appropriate narrator for the subject matter? We will take a deeper look at choosing a narrator later, but for now, just knowing that there is someone who can handle the text is another item you can check off your list or, if you think finding an appropriate reader presents an insurmountable hurdle, it may stop you from moving forward. Of course, if you are a narrator who is publishing the audiobook, you most likely plan to narrate it yourself and your search for the right voice is finished.

MAKING YOUR BUDGET

Once you determine your chosen book is adaptable to audio, you can start an inventory of the bevy of things that will help you to form your working budget.

See if you can get a word count from the book's publisher or the author, if you are licensing directly from her. A word count is just what it sounds like: the number of words in the manuscript. That number will help you to predict the final running time of your audiobook once you have recorded and edited it. I'll explain how to calculate this shortly. The running time is important for a number of reasons. First, it is rare these days to pay a narrator for each hour, or portion of an hour, spent in the recording studio or even preparing for the recording sessions. The per finished hour rate is much more common today. You might, instead, also pay a narrator a flat fee, if you can come to an agreement about what that fee should be. There is some security in knowing what your maximum out-of-pocket cost will be for the narrator, but if the running time is short, you may have overpaid. If you can afford it, that is not a bad thing. You have supported an independent contractor who is an artist. Another payment variation is that sometimes a narrator will work for no money up front and instead agree to a shared revenue from sales.

Now, suppose you make a deal with a narrator to record your audiobook for $225 per *finished hour*. A per finished hour (PFH) rate is often how narrators are compensated, as you have just learned. Knowing whether the audiobook will be four hours long or ten hours long helps you plan your budget. Will you be paying the narrator $900 or $2,250? That's a big difference in a budget.

We will get to other reasons you'll want to estimate the running time when we discuss studio time, sound editing, and mastering. Note that paying for services by the finished hour includes the total number of hours and minutes, so a running time of ten hours and twenty-three minutes will also include payment for the twenty-three minutes. Once you know your PFH rate, just divide it by sixty to find your per minute rate, and use that to calculate the minutes when a running time is not an even number of hours.

The rough rule of thumb in estimating running time is that 9,000 words are approximately equal to a finished hour. A book that has 65,000 words will likely have a running time of around seven hours and fifteen minutes. This is an educated guess. It could be six and a half hours if your narrator speaks quickly or it could be eight hours with someone who talks at a more deliberate pace but at least you are able to narrow your forecast of the running time to a likely window.

Sometimes you will not have access to the word count. There are ways to finesse this, but they provide less accurate estimations of projected running time. It's the difference between eyeballing the height of a window to fit it for drapes and actually taking a tape measure to it. Either way, you have a rough idea of what you need. One such alternate method is to try to get a page count. Unless you intend to record them, don't include the table of contents or the acknowledgments and footnotes and bibliographies and the like, typically found, if at all, at the back of the book. Now that you have an idea of the number of recordable pages, count the words on what looks like a typical page of the book or, alternatively, use the common gauge of 250 words per page. Multiply that number by the number of pages, unless some of the pages are blank or short, in which case you may adjust your multiplier accordingly. This will give you a very rough word count, but it will usually land you in the ballpark of the running time within an hour or two.

For the purposes of this lesson, you have determined your audiobook will have a running time of around ten hours. Here is an example of what goes into a typical budget for a projected ten-hour audiobook:

1. **RIGHTS TO THE BOOK**: The audio rights to a book will usually require payment of an advance against a royalty. We will take a close look at how to calculate the advance later. For now, let's say you have reached an agreement to pay an advance for the rights of $2,000.

2. **THE NARRATOR**: We have touched on the cost to hire a narrator. There are various ways to compensate your voice actor but ultimately what you choose will be whatever you and she can agree upon. Let's say you have agreed to a price of $250 per finished hour. You have estimated this will be a ten-hour book, so you put the sum of twenty-five hundred dollars into your budget for narration services.

One thing that impacts narrator pricing is SAG-AFTRA, which is a performers union. Many audiobook narrators are members of SAG-AFTRA, either solely because of their work in audiobooks or because they also perform in film and/or television or other voice-over work, such as for video games. The union has negotiated contracts with a number of audio publishers and producers, establishing minimum PFH and including a requirement that the producer contribute to the narrator's health and pension funds. That contribution is, typically, in an amount above the minimum recording rate. In some contracts, the PFH gross may include the contribution to health and pension and the narrator will receive a sum net of that contribution amount.

Unlike with commercials or video games, SAG-AFTRA does not have a national audiobooks agreement with uniform terms. Rather, it negotiates with individual publishers and producers. That means there is some flexibility in the terms, so long as the union feels the rates are consistent with similar-sized publishers nationwide. Also, importantly, there are generally no residuals or secondary payment obligations in audiobooks.

It is important for you to be aware of the union for a few reasons. First, if you are asked by a narrator to pay them union rates, now you know what they are talking about. If you are not a signatory to a SAG-AFTRA agreement, meaning that you have not entered into a contract with the union agreeing to specific pricing for hiring union talent, then you can still agree to pay union rates by using a *paymaster*. A paymaster is a third-party signatory to the union contract. They will make the payment to the union on your behalf for the project(s), and will add a surcharge for their services.

Narrators in the union are not forbidden to work with non-signatory publishers but some will turn down a job unless it includes contributions to their union health and retirement plans. As an alternative to using a paymaster, the union has a one-production-only agreement. Unlike its usual contracts, this is a way to do a single project or series with a union narrator. While there is a limit to how many times an employer can do this, it is a good way to get an initial experience of working with the union, without a long-term obligation.

If you start producing a fair number of audiobooks, SAG-AFTRA will be likely to hear about it from its members. Do not be surprised when the union approaches you to sign an agreement with them. Do not be surprised when, if you choose not to sign an agreement, they order a *work stoppage* for their members. The *work stoppage* means that union narrators will turn down any work you offer them unless and until you sign the agreement.

This leaves you with two choices: You can agree to sign it, or you can use nonunion narrators.

This is not necessarily a no-brainer. Depending on your views, you may think the easiest and best route for your future audiobooks is to work with nonunion talent. There are many, many audiobook narrators available, and you will not have a hard time finding some to work with you. This does mean that you are leaving out a large community of narrators who might otherwise be willing to work on your projects.

The other choice is to sign the agreement and be bound thereafter to pay the negotiated rates for voice-over talent. This opens up a large pool of narrator talent for you, including most of the best-known and most beloved narrators, who may have a following which can benefit your sales, to some extent.

If you have any questions about SAG-AFTRA contract terms or the signatory process, contact any of the audiobook representatives listed on the SAG-AFTRA website. They want you to be informed and are happy to speak to or email with you.

3. **EDITING:** You need to have the recording edited. Editors' pricing is a pretty vast spectrum so let's estimate a middle ground and presume you have found an editor to work with you for the price of $100 per finished hour. That is another $1,000 to put in your budget.

4. **QUALITY CONTROL, AKA QC:** You aren't finished with your budget yet. You need to have someone listen to the edited audiobook—someone to perform QC. This type of work is often in the ballpark of $25 to $40 per hour of running time. Let's budget $40 per hour. Better to come in under budget than to find you have gone over budget and don't have the money to finish your nearly finished project. At that PFH price, add $400 to your budget.

5. **COVER ART:** You will need to have cover art licensed from the publisher, from the artist, or designed by your own graphic artist, and a JPEG provided to you at whatever current specs are required by download sites, or for a CD, or other hard copy formatted audiobooks. We can just ballpark this at $500. It could be that the publisher will provide you with the art in usable JPEG format at no cost, or it could be your cost will be higher. For this rough budget, we'll settle on this sum as a likely scenario.

The reason you sometimes need to license the art from the artist is that the publisher may have only licensed the art for specific uses, and sublicensing for audiobook production might not be one of those paid-for uses.

Those are the main points of your production budget. When we add up these items, we find our budget for total production costs for this ten-hour finished running time project comes to $6,400.

Your budget, then, looks something like this:

- Rights to the book: $2,000
- Narrator: $250 per finished hour = $2,500
- Editor: $100 per finished hour = $1,000
- QC person: $40 per finished hour = $400
- Cover art design or license and jpeg: $500

You may wish to use a spreadsheet, an app, a legal pad. Any way you want to track your budget and your consequent actual costs will work. The main point is to have an idea of what your finished audiobook is likely to cost you and to keep on top of that. By doing this work up front, you'll be better prepared to deal with any changes to be made as a consequence of the actual expenses differing from your budgeted expenses, including any unexpected categories of expense which may arise. In this way, you will know what your outflow is even as your incurred costs are being incurred and then paid. The goal is to try to keep surprises to a minimum. Surprises do arise, though, so view your budget as a living document rather than as a finished form.

WHAT ELSE SHOULD BE IN YOUR BUDGET?

This budget doesn't include incidentals, such as water, coffee, snacks, and meals, but you can easily add a category for incidentals, determine what your maximum contribution to that can be, and adjust the total budget accordingly.

These numbers are purely fictional, but they are based on realistic fees. Any of the line items of any actual budget you design may be higher or lower, depending on with whom you work and from whom you license. What this sample budget does is give you a look at the essential categories you need to consider when looking at costs.

Another Very Essential Category: Producer and Director Fees

Are you going to produce and/or direct the audiobook yourself? If you are, and if you are new to the process, perhaps you should watch a pro and learn. I have spent time with new directors, at their requests, to teach them the ropes.

If you are not going to produce or direct, then your budget needs to accommodate payment for the producer and director. It used to be that the producer and director were often the same person, but now that there are numerous audiobook production companies, sometimes they use narrators who work at home without a director and sometimes they will hire a director to work in a studio with the narrator. A producer finds the director, the talent, the editor; books the studio; and farms the edited program out to a QC person or team.

What Does a Director Cost?

The director is used to being paid on a PFH basis and so calculating that cost is a matter of what that per finished hour rate is. I have heard of directors being paid as little as $100 per finished hour to as much as $300 or more per finished hour. This can depend on the prestige and experience of the director or it could depend on the complexity of the job. It may also depend on how much the director wants to work on the particular project. If it is of special interest to him, he may be willing to take a little less than his usual fee. When we plug these numbers into our sample budget, our range for a director is anywhere from $1,000 on the very low end to $3,000 on the higher, but still normal, end.

Remember that narrators working from home will not have a director. This will save you the cost of a director, but it may result in having more pickups after QC, as no one was with the narrator to point out errors. There are advantages and disadvantages to each process.

Certainly, if you are working with someone unused to recording audiobooks or someone who is a celebrity, you must have a director. It would be unfair to expect an inexperienced narrator to be capable of working alone and knowing all of the potential issues that can arise in that situation, such as researching pronunciations, knowing what recording format to use, listening for extraneous noise. With a celebrity narrator, it is good protocol to have a director. They are there to lend their talent and their cachet to the project, not to self-direct.

What Does a Producer Cost?

A producer may quote you a flat fee or she, too, may work for a PFH price. Ask her for her rates.

Two other ways to budget are to work with an outside producer and ask for an all-in bid, which is one price that includes all of the costs of producing a finished audiobook master recording. Alternatively, give them a price and see if they think they can meet it. They may give you a PFH rate that includes all the elements of the recording, bundled into one hourly rate. If the idea of spending $6,400 for a 10-hour audiobook, even before adding producer and/or director fees, is alarming to you, ask producers if they can do the project for whatever budget you have decided you can afford. Don't lowball someone just to lowball them, but often an established producer or director has a stable of talent they can call on to do some of the jobs for less than they would usually charge. Maybe someone (not just *any* someone, but a good narrator) can narrate it for $200 per finished hour rather than $250, saving you $500 on your ten-hour running time. Maybe the producer has a QC person who can do the job for $300, saving you another $100. You get the picture.

Anything you learn from this book is a guideline, and you can step over and under those guidelines if you are able to find good and experienced talent to work with you to save money without cutting corners that should not be cut. Quality matters.

One of the largest audiobook production companies in the United States, John Marshall Media, is owned by John Cheary. John and his team have produced thousands of audiobooks, including many for the large publishing houses, but they have produced for independent publishers as well. He has his own strong feelings about how to choose a narrator. He suggests that publishers should focus on finding a voice that has the ability to communicate the true feeling of the story by virtue of the narrator's ability to aurally express the author's meaning. He recommends that you get an audition from your prospective narrator, but don't just give them dialogue to record because, he says, "[Narrating] is how they can connect from their heart and their soul. How is that person going to connect with your text and the emotion in your words? The test of a good narrator is when nothing is going on (in the story), to find it. For example, someone is running. Why is the person running? Is he happy? Is he scared? A good actor will make a choice which will engage the listeners."

Usually the text will impart clues to what is happening, even in the quiet moments of the story, but John's point is that dialogue has its own imperatives, as the author will often give clues in the form of phrases such as "he whispered" or "she said nervously." The parts of the story which are without that sort of express instruction are where you can see how much a narrator can do with the text.

I have a caveat or two to add to this. First, auditions are usually no more than a few pages of the book; rightly so because it is hardly fair to expect a narrator to read more than that simply to try out for the gig. Because they are seeing just a small part of the overall work, they cannot be expected to know the broad strokes, much less the nuances, of the overall book. Do listen to their communicative abilities, but unless you have provided explicit instructions, do not automatically reject a prospective narrator on the basis that their intonation is incorrect if the tone you seek is not readily discernible from the pages provided for the audition.

Second, listening for heart in narration does not mean an over-the-top performance. The idea is to find the genuineness of the words, not to overplay them.

SUMMARY

This was a jam-packed chapter. You learned about assessing your book's feasibility for audio (including whether it is fiction or nonfiction, traditional or unorthodox in layout and style); how to piggyback on the visibility of other media; determining the likelihood of financial success of a project using assorted tools; thinking about narrators; budgeting; unions; paymasters; cover art; producers; directors; studios; and amenities for the narrator for food and drink. There is so much information that you may want to reread it or refer back to it as you become more steeped in audio publishing.

CHAPTER 4

Acquiring Audiobook Rights

Including Jessica's Top 3 Rules for Audiobook Publishers

COPYRIGHT (AGAIN? YES, AGAIN.)

Earlier, you learned a little bit about the copyright to the audiobook itself. Now we are going to discuss the copyright to the *source materials* for your audio program.

Audio rights include the bundle of rights that allow the audiobook producer to record and sell (or give away or sublicense) the recording or the right to produce a recording. If you do not have the rights that comprise audio rights, then you will need to acquire them prior to producing an audiobook. You may not need each of these enumerated rights to produce and sell an audiobook, but generally audio rights will encompass the right to sell, rent, license, or give away the program. You could have a contract that permits sales but disallows rentals or giveaways, for example.

One common situation today is that you have written a book you want to record. Although you are the author, there may be instances in which you do not own the copyright to the book or you do not own the audio rights. This can happen with a work performed under a contract by which you granted any copyright ownership you may have had in the book to another person or to a company. It can happen if you write the book as a work for hire, such as when you are an employee and what you have written is within the scope of your duties to your employer. It could be that you have assigned your copyright to a third party.

Regardless of how it has happened, if you do not own the copyright to your own book, then absent a written agreement specifically granting you the audio rights or, in the alternative, absent a written agreement specifying that the other party only has rights spelled out in that agreement and audio rights are not among them, you are not legally in a position to produce an audiobook for sale. This is because someone else has the right to do it and you would be infringing on those rights if you did so. All is not lost, however. You may be able to obtain those rights.

Even if you do own the copyright to your book, you may have already given away the audio rights, perhaps knowingly, perhaps unknowingly. Did you sign a contract with a publisher? Read that contract carefully or, better yet, have a publishing attorney read it for you to determine whether or not you still own your audio rights. If you do not, then the next section is just as applicable to you as it is to someone who is trying to license the rights to a book written by someone else.

HOW TO ACQUIRE AUDIO RIGHTS

Acquiring audio rights can be easy or it can be difficult. Sometimes it is impossible. What follows is an overview of how to do it.

The first thing you need in order to acquire rights is to know *what* rights you want to acquire. That sounds obvious, doesn't it? But if you have never acquired audio rights before, you may not know what you should be requesting from the rightsholder.

Most of the time you want an *exclusive agreement*. An *exclusive agreement* means that you will be the only one who can publish an audiobook based on the material you are licensing. This is not the case for public domain materials (defined below), since no one owns those rights and so the number of audiobook recordings based on such material cannot be limited. Just by way of example, take a look at any audiobook download site and count the number of offerings of *A Christmas Carol* by Charles Dickens.

Public Domain

Let's define the term *public domain*. It means not protected by copyright. A work that is in the public domain is, by definition, something anyone can use. That is why you will see numerous copies of older titles, such as books by the Brontë sisters, Jane Austen, or Mark Twain. There are a few things to be aware of even with public domain titles, however. We will talk about public domain and copyright more in Chapter 10.

WHAT RIGHTS AM I SEEKING?

Now that you know a little bit about copyright as it pertains to public domain, let's return to our discussion about which rights you are seeking when you license audio rights. If the object of your affection is not in the public domain, then, as we were discussing, you probably want exclusive rights.

In the earlier days of audiobooks, when abridged and unabridged productions were both likely, often those rights would be divided between two companies. One entity might obtain a license for the abridged rights and another company could publish the unabridged version. Sometimes both rights went to the same company. But now that abridged books are much less common, those rights are rarely divided. So, ask for exclusive rights. If the answer is no, ask why not. Do not ask as though you are challenging the licensor; just ask because you need to know whether to expect competition in the marketplace, albeit possibly in a different format and possibly the same format as whichever you are able to license. There usually is a good reason for the refusal to issue an exclusive license, such as the other rights are not held by the licensor or because they have already licensed some part of the audio rights. So, if you can't get a reasonable explanation from the rightsholder, consider whether this is someone with whom you want to work.

Nonexclusive Rights

Occasionally the rightsholder will issue a license to more than one licensee, even in the same format. For a good example of this, take a look at how many audiobook versions there are of *The Great Gatsby*. There are enough that you might assume it is in the public domain. It is not; not yet. The market seems to be able to accommodate multiple audio versions of this very popular book and the estate has authorized more than one publisher to release an unabridged audiobook recording.

This is illustrative of the important reason you want exclusive rights: You don't want to compete against another version of the same product. If you can only obtain *non*exclusive rights, be sure to be very clear who your competition is and find out who else has licensed the rights. That will help you to decide whether the nonexclusive rights will be worth enough to you to be able to coexist with another publisher of the same work. This will happen very rarely, so it isn't something to worry about unless and until it happens. Make your offer one for exclusive audio rights. I suggest that the same rights licensed to more than one company should go for less than an exclusive license but, as with all things, it depends on the popularity of the book. It may still be worth it to you to pay a good amount for the license, even for nonexclusive rights.

Now that you know what type of rights you seek, you need to know who owns the rights. Often your first outreach will be to the book's publisher. You will have figured out who that is either by looking at the book you have at hand to see who published it, finding the information online, or asking a research librarian at your local library.

At times, even finding out who the original publisher is can be a challenge. For example, you may have an edition of a book that was published by a company that only obtained paperback rights and so does not own any rights it can sublicense to you. Don't lose heart, though. Most likely, that publisher will be able to at least tell you from whom they licensed the rights they are exercising. You can then go to that publisher or the agent that granted those rights and ask them whether they hold the audio rights. If they do not, ask who does and whether they have contact information they can provide to you. The copyright page may even indicate something along the lines as "First published by Some Other Publisher, Inc." (not the name of a real publisher, so far as I am aware). But if the publisher to whom you have reached out *does* hold the audio rights, you then may inquire as to their availability for licensing. If the rights are held by the publisher and they are available for licensing, then you can inquire as to whether the publisher would be willing to license them to *you*. The word *you* is emphasized because just knowing that audio rights are available does not guarantee that the publisher will thrill to your inquiry and make a deal with you.

This is a good place to discuss *orphan works*. *Orphan works* means those books and other types of intellectual property for which you cannot find the rightsholder. Maybe the book is old, but not so old that it is out of copyright. Maybe the source material you seek is an article, a series of articles, or stories that were published in a pulp magazine in the 1950s. The magazine has gone out of business, and you have no one to whom you can logically turn to ask for audio rights.

There is one important thing to know about orphan works: Just because you cannot find the rightsholder does not mean you can publish an audiobook based on that work without obtaining a license to do so. You may not know who holds the rights, but you do know who *doesn't* hold them—you. Perhaps someday the laws regarding orphan works will change to allow greater access to rights held by persons or entities unknown. Congress does take a look at this issue from time to time because copyright is a matter of federal law, and so only Congress can make U.S. copyright laws. As of now, if you publish anything not in the public domain without a license from the rightsholder, you do so at the risk of being sued for copyright infringement. So, a word to the wise: Don't do it.

WHAT YOU AND SALLY FIELD HAVE IN COMMON

In 1984, Sally Field won the Oscar Award for Best Actress for her starring role in the film *Places in the Heart*. In her acceptance speech, she famously declared that she could no longer deny that the industry liked her.

If you are new to the audiobook publishing industry, it may be that a licensor will like you, but might turn down your request to license audio rights.

Let's look at a few reasons why a publisher may not wish to license the audio rights to you.

No Track Record

Publishers like to license subsidiary rights because they are a revenue generator. The large publishing houses even have a department dedicated to sublicensing. That department is called, naturally enough, the subsidiary rights department.

Subsidiary rights, another term you should know, are those rights that have been granted to the publisher, other than the publication of the text in full. I say *other than the publication of the text* because that is not a subsidiary right—that is the primary right, the original right from which other rights extend. Subsidiary rights, or sub rights, as they are often called, can include, among others, audio rights, foreign language rights, and first and second serial rights (the right to license part of the book for excerpting in a newspaper or magazine) and can be exploited by the publisher either by exercising the rights themselves, e.g. by publishing a paperback or audio edition of a book first published in whatever its original version is *or* by allowing another party to exploit those rights, such as licensing the audio rights to you or the paperback rights to another publisher. They may even let rights lie fallow, whether intentionally or for lack of a sublicensor. But a publisher wants to earn money or at least garner publicity for the underlying book when it chooses to license audio rights. To maximize the potential of these things happening, the publisher holding the audio rights most likely will want to license them to a company that has previously published audiobooks because established companies know who should receive review copies, and whether, when, and where to advertise. They may know how to obtain other forms of publicity. They have distribution in place. If you do not have that sort of track record, the publisher will, understandably, be reluctant to strike an arrangement with you.

We will discuss ways to combat publisher reluctance to license shortly.

Money

You are an independent publisher and you want to license the audio rights to a specific book or books. Do you have deep or shallow pockets? Are you offering a good advance and/or a good royalty figure? Or are you lowballing with a subpar advance or royalties? Not every publisher will require a healthy advance, especially if the book whose audio rights you are seeking did not sell many copies.

The audio rights to such a book are less valuable than those that sold a significant number of copies, so the publisher may be happy to generate any income at all through an advance from you. Before making an offer, do some hard math, whether or not math is your thing, because being a publisher means, to some extent, becoming familiar with numbers. Certainly being a *successful* publisher requires it. Here is why you need to do some math.

You need to determine how much of an advance is too much. Too little can also be a problem, but too much means you may not earn back enough to cover what you paid. Again, this is presuming that making a profit is part of your reason for publishing. If it is not part of your impetus to publish, then feel free to skip this section. If, however, like most of the world, you need to make more money than you spend, sketch out a few details. This includes the costs you will incur in obtaining the rights and the costs of producing the recording, plus the costs involved in manufacturing, if you are making hard copies of the audiobook. The costs, you will recall from Chapter 3, include recording, paying the narrator, and having someone edit the audiobook. You may have to pay a director or a producer. The editing costs often will include mastering the digital audiobook, which is necessary for getting it to the download sales venues or ready for CD replication. We will get into what mastering means in Chapter 8: Nuts and Bolts.

Try to get the editor to include mastering in the price you and she agree to, but know that some audio editors charge extra for that service or may not do mastering themselves at all. It is important to know up front whether your fee to the editor includes mastering. I once made the mistake of assuming the editor was going to deliver a mastered audiobook, only to learn that they expected an additional fee to master it after it was edited.

Next, don't forget to include any costs for preparing cover art. Even if you only distribute the title digitally and forego hard copy, you still must provide download sites with a digital file of an audiobook cover, typically in JPEG format.

While we are on the topic of cover art, it is essential to understand that when you license rights to the underlying material, you are not necessarily also licensing rights to use the cover art. We talked about this briefly in Chapter 3, but here is some more detail. The art is not automatically included. You will either have to develop your own or ask to license the existing cover art. It is possible to, and I do recommend you do, ask for those rights to be included in your license of audio rights. In the case of both large or small companies, whether or not they will include the art as part of your licensing deal often depends on whether they actually own those rights themselves. Sometimes book covers are designed in-house, but many times the publisher will have paid a third party to design the book jacket. They may not have obtained the right to sublicense the art in their agreement with that artist or graphic designer.

If the publisher does have the right to license the art to you, they sometimes will make it available for free, or they may ask for payment for the art in addition to the licensing fee for the audio rights. Or they may refer you to the graphic designer, who will then want a fee. Sometimes those fees are high. So again, be sure you are comfortable with your budget. When the book cover art isn't available to you or is too costly to license, you can rest assured that many audiobook jackets vary from the hard copy book art, and many of them look good. If you do develop your own cover art, make it look as good as the audiobook sounds. You must be competitive in the marketplace, and just as your audiobook must sound as good as one from a major publisher, its cover art, even if just a small JPEG on a digital download site, must look professional. Occasionally, albeit rarely, the art really defines the book—it is iconic as a representation of the book. In that case, go ahead and pay whatever it is you can stomach paying to license that cover.

Unless you are licensing the audio rights as a buyout, meaning there will be no royalties to be calculated and paid, try to include the art fee as part of the advance. The reason for this is so that your recoupable advance is larger than if the two fees are paid separately, in which case the art licensing fee might not be recoupable. Alternatively, try to have the licensor agree that the fee for the art *is* also recoupable.

To understand what that means, we have to talk about *recoupable fees*. When an advance is *recoupable*, it means that before you owe royalties, you first get to earn back what you have spent. In most audiobook licensing contracts, the only thing recoupable is the advance.

Here's an example. You pay $1,000 to license the audio rights to a book, and you have agreed to pay a royalty of 10 percent of revenue received. You receive revenue of $10,000, and so you are at breakeven for the advance: 10 percent of $10,000 equals $1,000, which is what you paid as the advance. Every dollar you earn from this point on will earn a royalty of ten cents for the licensor.

Now let's suppose you were required to pay a fee for the right to use the cover art. We will imagine you paid $250. If this is a recoupable fee, then you need not pay royalties until you have earned $12,500 because 10 percent of that is $1,250 and your total recoupable outflow is $1,250, consisting of the $1,000 paid for the audio rights and the $250 for the art. If the $250 for the art is *not* recoupable, then anything above $10,000 will begin to earn a royalty for the rightsholder.

As always, this is just an example. Your numbers will likely differ from project to project, but the concept of recouping before beginning to owe a royalty will remain the same, unless you've made a buyout agreement.

Your budget might include marketing costs, such as advertising or promotion, if any, in your calculations, but for many small or new audiobook publishers, the marketing and promotion budget is slim to nonexistent. Although you may not have a budget for promotion, it is you, the publisher, who is responsible for banging the drums to let the public know your audiobook is out in the world. This is not the responsibility of your distributor or of the retailers. It is part of what publishers must do. You can probably be creative and come up with a number of ideas of how to promote your audiobook. To help get you started, there are some ideas about this a little later in the book.

Don't underestimate the importance of social media. Build a following for your company or even for the audiobook itself. If your narrator has a large following, ask him to tweet or post something about the audiobook, preferably more than once and with a link to a purchase point. Ask the author to do the same, if you are in a position to ask that of them.

Calculating Breakeven

Once you have figured in all of your likely expenses, including rights, narrator, studio, possibly producer and director, editor, and cover art, you will have a rough idea of what your hard costs will be, excluding manufacturing and warehousing, sales and shipping costs. Take the sum of those estimated costs to give you an idea of how much money you will have to earn from sales of the program just to break even on the project. You can work with these figures to see how much you can allocate to the advance.

Pricing Your Audiobook

But there is still more to this calculation. In order to be able to determine whether you believe you will be able to at least break even with the sales of the audiobook, if not make a profit, you need to know your suggested retail price. How do you determine that?

There are a number of ways to decide the retail price of an audiobook. It used to be fairly standard to determine how long the running time of the audiobook is or will be and then compare it to the price of programs in the same or similar genre with similar running times. That is still an effective method of deciding what to charge. Take a look at the price, or range of pricing, of similar programs. That will give you a ballpark of the range in which your price should fall.

Another way some publishers choose the price is to pull it out of thin air. This is not very scientific but sometimes a publisher feels the worth of the program is not based on its running time. I agree that sometimes this is the case. If the price is much higher than similar audiobooks on the market, there must be something exceptional about the program: either the content or the delivery of the content must spectacularly distinguish itself from similar works. An example of this might be if you somehow obtained a recording of a speech by Abraham Lincoln (quite a feat, as recording devices were not yet in use during his lifetime). In that circumstance, the copies you could create from that recording would have a value that likely would be based on the rarity of hearing Lincoln's voice, rather than the length of the recording. This is clearly a fanciful example, but it is fanciful in order to make the point that an exceptional audiobook warranting premium pricing is a rare thing.

You will also find some publishers charging what seems a high price for programs that have content specific to an industry or perhaps containing information from someone with expertise in his field. These may carry a premium in pricing for a reason similar to the made-up example of a recording by Lincoln: The price reflects the unusually valuable content. Hence, you will sometimes see recordings priced at many multiples of what similar audiobooks, in terms of run time, are priced at, if the seller believes there is a market for these expensive programs.

Before you convince yourself that your program is indeed worthy of a lofty price, consider your prospective audience. First of all, will they be able to afford it, or will the price become a barrier to purchasing it? Second, is it really the case that your content or the voice talent is so valuable that a high price will not deter sales?

Back to my example involving Abraham Lincoln's recording: *That* is a rare and exceptional program. Similarly, someone like Zig Ziglar, the late motivational speaker, could charge a premium for some of his programs, but that is because he was acknowledged as an expert in his field and was a dynamic speaker, and his audio recordings held out the promise of teaching its listeners to become tops as salespeople.

Thinking of Zig Ziglar brings me to another place where high price points may work well: *back-of-the-room sales.* This term refers to selling your audio programs at events where you have been featured, either as a speaker addressing a group or in some other manner. This is something Zig Ziglar did well. I was fortunate to see him at a conference, and he held the audience's rapt attention. They were able to purchase Mr. Ziglar's recordings right there at the event.

Back-of-the-room sales may have a high retail price point. You have a captive audience who, presumably, are interested in hearing what *you* have to say.

Again, your success in naming a high price depends on your visibility in your field and what you are imparting to your listener. If the information contained in the program is considered invaluable to the audience, such as Zig Ziglar's techniques for getting in the door to try to sell something and then how to close the sale once you are in, then you can try offering your back-of-the-room sales at a high price. Or, you may opt to do back-of-the-room sales but consider using a more competitive price point for programs of your audiobook's length and genre.

A caveat: If you are selling both hard copy and digital downloads of your program, you will want to have two different price points. The download is often priced lower than the hard copy audiobook, in large part because of the out-of-pocket costs that go into manufacturing physical products, e.g. CDs or vinyl or whatever substance your hard copy audiobook is composed of, as well as the costs of packaging, shipping, storage, sales reps, and so on. All the things that used to be a barrier to entry are still expensive when used in lieu of or in addition to download sales. Downloads can sell for less than physical goods because there is no packaging, no sales person, no shipping, and no warehousing, other than on a server. Still, there is an audience for customers who like to hold an audiobook in their hands more than or in addition to downloads.

If you have estimated sales based on the tools we discussed, then by multiplying that number by the retail price, less an average discount from retail, let's say fifty percent, you will have your estimated gross income for that title. An additional common rule of thumb is that most of the sales of an audiobook will take place in the first twelve months after publication.

You will learn more about discounts to wholesale and retail customers in Chapter 9. A key thing to know, though, is that neither the 10 percent rule from Chapter 3 nor the twelve-month rule you just learned will give you a fully reliable number. They may help you come up with some rudimentary sales projections, though, and that will help you compare projected income against projected costs. If that turns out to be a number in the black, you may have something. If it looks as though the title will be in the red, then consider whether that works for you or whether you need the title to contribute to your company's bottom line. If you do, does that mean you cannot publish it? Is it too late to back away from the deal without harming your standing with the licensor? Or will you earn back enough of the outlay to make it worthwhile to move forward to preserve relationships, grow your publishing catalog, and your business reputation? These are all calculations each publisher faces and each decides based on their own needs and values.

Reputation

You may be known and you may have money, but you may not be someone to whom the publisher wants to license rights. You have no right to demand that someone license audio rights to you. The licensor's reluctance to enter into an agreement with you could be because you have a reputation for not providing accounting statements on time or for making late payments, if at all. It could be because you are known for publishing poor-quality books or producing other poor-quality goods. Perhaps you have a reputation for being litigious.

For any of these or other reasons, the publisher may not wish to have their book associated with you or your company. Sometimes this can be overcome by offering enough money as an advance that subsequent accountings and payments are less important because the upfront money is so substantial. That may work with some publishers, but it will not work with all of them.

Rights Hoarding

I've made this term up, so far as I'm aware. What I mean by it is that sometimes rightsholders will not license audio rights even though they are not planning to record an audiobook. They may be hoarding them for different reasons: the belief the rights will become more valuable in the future; a daydream that they might produce the audio version themselves some day; unfamiliarity with the process of licensing audio rights; dislike of audiobooks. A famous example of the latter is J.D. Salinger, the author of, most famously,

The Catcher in the Rye. During the author's lifetime, he did not permit his work to be recorded. Now that he is no longer alive, perhaps that will change and we will see audiobook versions of his books. There may be other reasons for rights hoarding. Whatever the reason, in those instances your offer will fall on deaf ears, regardless of your reputation or the amount of money you are able to offer.

JESSICA'S NUMBER ONE RULE FOR AUDIOBOOK PUBLISHERS

You've just learned some reasons you may not be able to license the rights to an audiobook. To help you with such situations, here comes my Number One Rule for Audiobook Publishers: *Never fall so much in love with a book that you can't walk away from it.*

I will digress a little from the nuts and bolts to impart some wisdom (really!). You have to be able to walk away from a negotiation for audio rights, no matter how much you had hoped to publish the audiobook. Again, the exception to this rule is if you don't care about making money or breaking even. Then you may continue to try to throw dollars at someone who is rejecting your offers. For most people, however, audio publishing is both a labor of love *and* a business. So enjoy yourself, but be practical. Sometimes audio rights just aren't worth the amount being sought by the rightsholder.

If the numbers don't add up, don't let your love for a project prod you into paying more than you should; more than you should means more than it is worth; more than it is worth means you should go back to the section that explained how to determine your break-even point.

The other reason to live by my Number One Rule for Audiobook Publishers is not about money. It is about your heart and dedication to the idea of a specific project. It hurts to be told no when you have a lovely idea in your imagination of what a wonderful audiobook you could create and how much the property means to you. If you can remember not to let any one project consume your emotions, which you may at times confuse for business sense, then receiving an unwavering no will be less hurtful.

Instead, pick yourself up. One project was turned down, so look ahead to the next one. Indeed, you may not always know why you were unable to obtain the rights you sought. Ultimately, it doesn't matter. Move on.

OVERCOMING RELUCTANCE TO LICENSE TO YOU

Now that you know some reasons publishers may say no to your inquiry, much less an offer, there are things you can do to try to change a maybe or a no to the yes you seek.

One method we have already discussed is offering more money. Another is bidding a lot of money right off the bat (not my recommendation for an opening gambit). Negotiating is a game of strategy, and the problem with giving your all in the first offer is that you have nowhere else to go when the other party comes back to you and asks for more money, or more anything.

You may think it is unfair that you were up-front and made an honest offer. Here's one thing I have learned about negotiating contracts: People like to feel that they have improved upon an initial offer. This is a lesson in strategy. I use this and I think it is a good tool in negotiations; it's one that most experienced negotiators also employ. When I make an offer, or when I send a contract, I know where in the offer or the contract are some terms that I can back away from so that the other side feels like they've made progress. If they are willing to accept what you've presented, so much the better. But you should know where the points are in your offer, or in your contract once you've made the offer, where you can give in, whether a little or a lot. When the other side comes back to you and says, "We can't agree to this clause," you need to know if it's a deal breaker for you or if it isn't. So, I always like to let the other side feel as though they have done something good for whomever they represent.

Often that means coming in with a lower advance than where you are willing to cap. A caveat: It doesn't help you to come in and say, "Hey, I'm going to be really honest with you. This is the offer I'm making. This is all we can do." Nobody believes you. Everyone is going to suggest that you think about it some more, and they're going to counter. They're going to ask you to increase the offer. So, don't lead with your best shot even if you have reason to think the other side is going to go for it. Give them a chance to return with a counterproposal and make sure that you have left room for yourself to negotiate up, because often that is how you get to a win-win.

Build in what I call *give points* to your offer—places where you can say *okay* to changes requested by the other party. Whether it is the term, the advance, the royalty: Give someone a chance to do better than your first offer. This is a powerful psychological tool to keep in your pocket. You get the rights you seek; they get an improved deal. Negotiations call for a bit of acting, in a way. All the world's a stage, etcetera. For those of you who don't recognize that mangled quote, I borrowed it from Shakespeare's *As You Like It*. Yes, Shakespeare's works are in the public domain.

Don't take this technique to mean you should lowball the licensor on every point of the agreement. It is called an agreement for a reason. If your terms are so onerous that even improving them will still make for a bad deal, there is not much to entice someone to say yes. You will learn to finesse this over time: You will get to know what parts of your contract have room to give and what parts do not.

Strategic Partners

Another tactic you can try in an effort to swing a no to a yes is to partner or somehow combine your talents with that of someone or some company already known and trusted by the rightsholder. That may be enough to relax the rightsholder's grip.

Maybe you have become friendly with the author and the author will back you (not financially) by telling the publisher they want you to have the audio rights. That doesn't obligate the publisher to agree to allow you to publish the audiobook, but it doesn't hurt to have the author in your corner.

These are just a couple of suggestions of how to sweeten your appeal to someone who has no idea who you are. You may think of something else to convince the licensor that although you are new to audio publishing, you are a good bet for them. Have something to back up that claim—your ability to distribute through a tried-and-true source, a promise of a purchase in bulk from a customer, a high-profile narrator. Use whatever you have up your sleeve that may help them see you as a desirable prospective licensee.

If you are unknown to the person or company holding the rights you covet, do yourself a favor and prepare an email or talking points for a telephone conversation that will fully support your claim to be the right home for those rights.

A final suggestion: There is nothing wrong with being frank with the publisher on this point. Ask them to tell you what you can do to change their maybe or their no to a yes.

They Still Said No

Sometimes it is hard to walk away from a project. You really, really, *really* have your heart set on it. That's okay. It happens to most of us at one time or another. You will have twinges of regret. You may feel sad or let down. You will get over it. You will. Remember my Number One Rule for Audiobook Publishers: Never fall so much in love with a book that you can't walk away from it. They said no and you are disappointed. Unless this was the only project you wanted to produce, then go on to the next one and see if there are any takeaways to be learned. If it is the only project you want to produce, then you have little recourse other than to let the disappointment heal.

JESSICA'S NUMBER TWO RULE OF AUDIOBOOK PUBLISHING

My Number Two Rule of Audiobook Publishing is that *a no is better than no answer at all because at least you know where you stand.*

JESSICA'S NUMBER THREE RULE OF AUDIOBOOK PUBLISHING

This is a good place to remind you to be gracious and polite. You never know when someone you deal with today is someone you will be dealing with again in the future. Even if you never deal with them again, they may let others know about how you comported yourself. Do not leave a poor impression. There's no reason to act badly in this situation, anyway. Be nice. Some of those who listened to a webinar I did with Karen Commins about licensing audiobooks in 2016 will remember these important words:

Don't be a jerk! We can dress this up and say don't be difficult or don't be obnoxious. No matter what you call bad behavior, no one wants to work with a jerk. The Number Three Rule of Audiobook Publishing should be easy for you to carry out: Don't be a jerk.

I recently saw someone coming into a grocery store just as I was leaving. I laughed out loud at the words on his T-shirt because it said that same thing, albeit with much more colorful language than the word *jerk*. Whatever word you choose to call poor behavior, just don't engage in it.

WHAT IF THEY SAY YES?

Congratulations, you have obtained audio rights! Now you need to memorialize that agreement. Memorializing an agreement means to put it in writing. You will get detailed explanations of the contract terms in the next chapter, but for now, here are a few important pieces of information.

Standard Operating Behavior in Contract Negotiations

It is normal for there to be a back-and-forth exchange in both the negotiation for rights and the contract memorializing that agreement, so don't feel as though either of those are abnormal or that they are affronts to your integrity or your contract. It is entirely par for the course. That's how contracts become a memorialization of the meeting of minds.

The Contract

There is a contract included at the back of this book. It is just one format among many audiobook licensing agreements that publishers currently use. The purpose of including one is to familiarize you with key clauses you are likely to encounter, whatever contract you receive. We will examine these clauses one by one in the next chapter. For now, here are a few highlights.

When you license audio rights from a major publisher (by *major publisher* I mean the big ones, such as Penguin Random House, Simon & Schuster, HarperCollins, MacMillan, Hachette, and the like), most of the time they will issue a contract to you.

They have a form agreement and, usually, they prefer to use it. You should read it carefully to make sure it conforms with the terms to which you believe you have agreed. If you find discrepancies, point them out, politely, to the publisher. Mistakes happen. So do misunderstandings. Either one of you may have meant something other than how it was interpreted by the other.

It is also important to understand the terms in the contract you are signing because while you may have a good idea of some of the important items, such as advance and royalty, there will be boilerplate language, which means the usual terms of the publisher, included in the agreement, and you will need to understand their meaning in order to comply with them. Failure to comply with the terms of the agreement could result in default, or breach of contract, which could result in the *reversion of rights* for which you have paid.

Reversion of rights means that any rights you may have received under the agreement are terminated and revert to the publisher. It doesn't matter that you paid for those rights. You also agreed to do a number of other things by signing the contract.

If you license rights from a smaller publisher, or from an agent or an individual, they may ask *you* to provide the agreement. It is equally important in this scenario to make sure you understand the contract you send them because it is possible that the rights-holder may challenge some of the terms or ask you to explain what you mean by a clause. It is equally essential that you know what the terms mean so that, again, you understand what your own rights and obligations are.

As with major publishers, in the case of licensing rights from a major literary agency, they may have their own form agreement they prefer to use. Sometimes they will ask you for your contract instead. Once they have seen it, they will let you know which terms they want to include that are not in your agreement and which terms in your agreement they wish to delete. If so, see whether the addition of the new clauses or the deletion of any clauses is acceptable to you. Or, they may agree to keep the clauses but to change the wording in some of them. If they proffer a change in wording, go over the new language carefully with your literary attorney to see whether it changes the meaning of the clause. If it does, consider whether that new meaning is acceptable to you or not, and whether you need to include language with what the previous meaning was, as well. If the new language is not acceptable, let the other side know that and your reasons. For example, a contract you send states that you may choose not to send accounting statements in any period for which there were no sales of the audiobook. The agent deletes that option. You now are required to send accounting statements even for sales periods for which there were no sales. That is not unreasonable, but it does change the clause. Similarly, if a rightsholder changes the word *may* to *shall*, that changes the meaning of a clause because in legalese, the word *may* is permissive while the word *shall* is mandatory. Anything the contract says you shall do, you must do. Anything you may do is your choice to do or not do.

Territory

Let's move on to another key part of your agreement: the territory. Territory means the parts of the world where you are contractually permitted to sell the audiobook.

Many contracts limit your territory. There are versions of standard territories for contracts, but before we get there, it is important to know that a rightsholder cannot grant you anything to which they, themselves, do not have the rights.

What do I mean by that? Territory is a good example to use to explain this concept. You want worldwide audio rights to *The World's Best Book*. You have made an offer, the publisher agreed to license it to you based on the advance and royalty rate, and the fact that you conducted negotiations respectfully. *Oh, no!* You forgot to discuss territory! The contract arrives, and it grants you the right to publish the audiobook in the English language in the United States, Canada, and the Philippines.

You go back to the publisher. You tell them that you intended the offer to encompass worldwide rights. *So sorry,* you are told. *We cannot grant worldwide rights to you because we only have U.S., Canada, and the Philippines in our own agreement for the underlying book.* It had not crossed your mind that they couldn't agree to what you had thought went without saying.

It doesn't go without saying. Nothing does. So make sure your offer includes the territory you seek.

Is the discrepancy between your belief and the publisher's understanding a deal breaker? Like so much in life, it depends. Would the bulk of the sales likely be in the U.S. anyway? If so, you will be fine with the territory. That's one factor. Each case is different. If, however, an unexpected contract term is a deal breaker for you, you can ask to back out of it because of the misunderstanding.

Make sure the contract specifies the language in which you plan to publish. Most licenses will be for English language rights. Do you intend to publish in another language? Are you going to hire a translator? That is not a very likely scenario for most audio publishers, but maybe it is realistic for your company. Are you planning to sublicense foreign language rights and let another company come out with the German or French audiobook? Does the contract grant you that right, or at least not restrict you from doing that?

Most of the time you will seek the rights in just the language or languages in which you truly intend to publish. There may be circumstances in which you do want to acquire rights for more languages than just English. If so, be clear with the licensor that you are seeking rights to English as well as additional languages.

It can get complicated because foreign language audiobook rights may have been previously licensed with a foreign rights deal for the book, so your claim to those rights could be at odds with someone else's claim. For example, a bestseller in the United States may be licensed to a publisher in Germany, and, along with the book license, the German publisher may have also obtained audio rights. Thus, those would not be available to you. In that case, you will seek the German audiobook rights from the German publisher and make sure that the rights you seek include the right to use their translation. They may not be able to grant you the right to do your own translation, anyway.

I think there is relatively little danger of a major publisher mistakenly granting you foreign language rights that have actually been licensed to another company, but it may occasionally be something to be aware of when you are negotiating with those who have limited experience in licensing audio rights and seem unsure as to what rights they hold.

Maybe you are seeking foreign language rights from the get-go. You may want to publish the Spanish-language version of a book. Again, be aware the publisher can only license to you those rights it actually controls. You find out who controls those rights in a similar manner to finding out who controls English-language audiobook rights—the threshold issue we discussed early on. If the publisher does not control the rights to the language you wish to license, ask who does control those rights. They should be able to point you back to whomever they obtained the book rights from or to whomever they licensed the book in that language.

If you do hold foreign language audiobook rights and manage to sublicense to a third party, recognize there will need to be a translation made; be clear in your contract to that licensee that the responsibility for the translation lies with them, not with you, unless you already have a translation, such as when you are the book publisher yourself and have published in that foreign language. If you are not the original rightsholder and have obtained audio rights by license, be clear in the contract from your licensor that you can make this sort of sublicensing arrangement. I recommend that you also have a clause that allows you the approval rights over the translation. You can always waive your right to review and approve the translation later if you are unable to understand the language or, better, you can hire someone you trust to read the translation and let you know if it is good. To do that, they need the original to compare it to, of course. It could be that your agreement with the original licensor requires that any sublicenses in languages other than English be approved by them, or that the translation is submitted to them for approval. Again, this entire scenario is not currently likely, but as worldwide audio rights become more valuable—they are increasing in value and will become even more valuable—this is another thing to tuck away to think about when the time is ripe.

SUMMARY

In Chapter 4 you have learned how to acquire audio rights, how to try to turn a no into a yes, and how to handle a no that remains no. You were introduced to my first three rules for audiobook publishing. Do you remember them? Rule Number One: Never fall so in love with a book that you cannot walk away from it. Rule Number Two: A no is better than no answer. Rule Number Three: Don't be a jerk.

So far, so simple. Let's keep going.

CHAPTER 5

Contracts

They're Not Boring, They're Essential!

We have just talked about acquiring rights but have not covered in detail the rest of what goes into contracts. Welcome to your tutorial on what the contract should say and what the terms mean. It is absolutely critical that you know and understand what you are signing, as well as what clauses should or should not be in any agreement you are offered or that you prepare. How can you adhere to the terms of an agreement you don't understand, or ensure the other party is compliant, if you don't fully comprehend what you have each agreed to do?

The main pieces of an audio rights licensing agreement include the following, or similar, clauses.

INTRODUCTORY CLAUSE

Most contracts start out with a paragraph identifying the parties to the agreement. This paragraph may include the legal names of each party and the type of organization it is (an individual, a corporation, an LLC, a DBA, and so forth). It may also include where the company was formed, stating, for example, The World's Best Audiobook Publisher, a California LLC. The clause will often include the address of each party, although sometimes the address appears later, either in a notice provision or on the signature page. The introductory paragraph usually gives a shortened name for each party, to be used throughout the rest of the contract. It doesn't matter which party is named first. For example, the paragraph may say "This Agreement ('Agreement') is entered into between The World's Best Audiobook Publisher ('Licensee') and The Rightsholder ('Licensor')." The words in parentheses, often with quotation marks, in this instance *Licensee* and *Licensor*, are the words that will be used to identify each party throughout the rest of the contract. Some contracts may use identifying words other than *Licensor* and *Licensee*. What you are called is less important than the consistent use of the designated terms. You don't want to use varying words to describe each party later in the document because that will make it confusing to understand who is charged with what responsibility under the contract. This manner of identifying each party is short and sweet and also common in contracts. You will see this used in the sample agreement I've included, where the appellations are *Publisher* and *Rightsholder*, rather than *Licensor* and *Licensee*, as it is an agreement to acquire audio rights from the rightsholder.

Here is one more thing to know about parenthetical terms that use quotation marks: They are not limited to identifying the parties. Wherever used in a contract, they are deemed the *defined terms* in a contract. You may see other words or phrases in the contract set out this way. This does not mean all words in parentheses are defined terms, as there are other reasons to use parentheses; but if you see parentheses following a name or term not previously used in the contract and with a name, likely capitalized and possibly in quotation marks, that is almost sure to be a *defined term*. That means wherever you see that word or phrase in the contract, it will have the meaning set out in the paragraph in which you first meet those words.

Once introductions are out of the way, the nitty-gritty follows. Let's first look at the term—not the terms of the deal but, rather, the duration of the contract.

TERM

The *term* of the agreement defines the time period during which the contract is in effect. When do the rights begin and when do they terminate?

What I usually suggest is that you try to get a term of at least ten years. While we have already said that many audiobooks have most of their sales during the first year of release, that doesn't mean the revenue stream ends after twelve months. You have put money and effort into producing the audiobook. You want the longest possible time in which to both recoup your costs and make a profit. The longer the term, the better the chances of increased revenue.

We talked about recoupment earlier. It means earning back the money you have advanced. In regard to paying royalties, you recoup the advance before royalties begin to accrue. Similarly, in recouping your costs in publishing an audiobook, you are earning back enough to cover what you spent. This uses similar language to recouping your advance, but recouping your costs is an internal matter and it means the point at which your audiobook has moved out of the red and into the black.

You will get pushback on a ten-year term from some rightsholders. Ten years seems like a long time to the person who is licensing the rights to you. During that time, they may have to give up other opportunities that may be more worthwhile. Or they may have other reasons to want the license to be for a limited time period. You will hear all sorts of suggestions for the term of a contract, but I never like to agree to less than a seven-year term and absolutely no less than five years.

I have said that there are exceptions to every rule. If John Grisham offers you the audio rights to his next book for only one year, don't say no because I told you not to accept terms shorter than five years. Sometimes opportunities come along, although that one is unlikely. If you recognize an opportunity, remember that rules are not one size fits all. They tend to be one size fits most.

It is important to know when the term of the agreement ends. Regardless of the length of the term, it is beneficial to you to have the yardstick by which the termination date is measured begin upon the publication date of your audiobook rather than the date the contract is signed. It may take you a year or more to produce the work and get it to market. While audiobooks often can be produced quickly, sometimes things hit snags: you were waiting for a particular narrator whose schedule wouldn't open until much later down the road; the artwork wasn't ready; the distribution you had in place went away and you had to find a new distributor. Many things can interfere with your envisioned release date. If it happens, it is reassuring to know that you still have the full contract term ahead of you rather than having lost some of the time of sales potential while awaiting the confluence of events leading to your publication date.

Publishers and agents know this, of course, so some of them may feel it is to their benefit to have the term begin to run from the date of the contract. Push back on that if you can. If you can't, then either get the audiobook to market quickly, or in time to coincide with a specific event, if that is germane to your project: for example, the release of a major motion picture based on the book. The longer you wait to publish, the less time you will have to earn sales revenue.

Some publishers will look at things differently and want you to have the opportunity to maximize sales since they will reap the economic benefit of that, if the advance earns out. They may be willing to agree to the termination period starting to run from the date of publication, not from the date of signing the agreement.

Along these same lines, some publishers and agents will want a clause that guarantees publication within a particular time frame.

Let's say you agree to publish within one year of signing the agreement or the rights will revert. Or it may be an eighteen-month window or a six-month window. It can be any period of time to which the parties agree. The important point is that the penalty for failing to publish within that specified amount of time may be a reversion of the rights for which you paid. I say *may be* rather than *will be* because you might be able to obtain a waiver of the reversion from the licensor, depending on the reason for the delay and, quite frankly, whether the licensor wants to keep the contract alive or not.

WHO GETS WHAT?

The contract will say what rights are being given by which party. When you acquire audiobook rights, you are exchanging something of value of yours for something of value of theirs. They are giving you the right to publish an audiobook, and you are giving them a financial interest in that project.

You may be asking for additional things and somewhere in the agreement you need to specify those things. For example, you will want the licensor to provide you with a copy of the manuscript, preferably the final, recordable version, emailed to you in PDF or Word format rather than hard copy, although a hard copy or two may come in handy, too. If the rights are to an older book, the licensor may not have an electronic manuscript. If a physical book is all you can get, then unless it is a valuable book, such as a rare first edition, see if you can take it apart, photocopy the pages, and either scan them to make your own PDF or at least have separate photocopied pages from which the studio team can work. The team will have to be mindful of paper noise, to keep it to a minimum so as not to affect the recording.

You will have asked the licensor about cover art, which we have discussed.

The licensor may require approval over your choice of a narrator. If they request that, it should be because their contract with the author requires it. It is fair for you to ask why they want the right of approval. Do it politely. As the audio publisher, it should be up to you to make choices based on what you think will be best for the audiobook. As licensor of the rights, they may have an interest in those same things.

Sometimes you and the publisher will agree to some things that they will not want to put into the contract. It could be that they don't want to set a contractual precedent, or it could be that company policy doesn't allow it. That may be acceptable; I've had to agree to that before. If this comes up and you are unsure whether it is workable for you, consult with an attorney, preferably a literary attorney, and even more preferably, an attorney knowledgeable about audiobook contracts.

FINANCIAL TERMS

Finances are one of the most important parts of the contract. We have talked about the advance, and you will include a clause which specifies what that agreed amount is.

(i) Buyout

Earlier in the book, I briefly mentioned *buyouts*. Sometimes you will pay money as a lump sum payment. That is called a buyout or what some publishers call a flat fee. The buyout is usually paid at one time and upon signing of the contract, just as is an advance against royalties, but a buyout means you do not have to pay royalties. It means the money you pay up front is the only money you will pay. You are buying out the rights with your one-time payment, for the term of the agreement. A buyout may be attractive to the rightsholder because it may be a larger amount than what an advance would have been. It is a guarantee of a specific sum of money, while an advance against royalties is a risk. I cannot recall whether I have ever negotiated a contract that was a buyout. If it is of interest to you, you can give it a try, but most licensors seem to prefer to stick to the tried-and-true formula of advance and royalties.

(ii) Royalties

In that financial terms clause, include the agreed royalties.

As we discussed, sometimes there will be no advance, but rather a royalty from dollar one. By *dollar one* I mean the very first sales money you see. In a deal of this nature, you are saved the expense of money up front to license the material and in lieu of that, you calculate the royalty on *all* sales. There is no recoupment because there is no advance to recoup.

Regardless of whether you have paid an advance or are paying royalties from first dollar earned, you need to determine what royalty rates you should offer. Part of this depends on what the other party requires of you, but there are certain ballpark royalty rates that are within industry norms. Still, royalty rates do vary broadly, even among different formats of the same audiobook. A royalty for hard copy, whether that is CD or vinyl (newly popular again) or any other hard copy format, will generally be something like 10, 12, and 15 percent, if you need to escalate your royalty rates.

Why would you need to escalate royalties? This is a carrot to the rightsholder. You are agreeing that if the audiobook performs well, by which I mean *sells* well, you will share the benefits of that great sales performance by increasing the royalty rates. Your royalty agreement may look something like this: Ten percent (10%) for the first five thousand (5,000) units sold, twelve percent (12%)

for the next five thousand (5,000) units sold, and fifteen percent (15%) of all sales thereafter.

Your steps may be bigger or smaller, based on sales of ten thousand (10,000) units or twenty-five hundred (2,500) units, or whatever you and the rightsholder agree to. There is no magical number to step up royalty rates. For your benefit, try to space them out as widely as possible but not so far out that the step increase is meaningless to the licensor.

Just what is that royalty a percentage of? Well, you do not want it to be a percentage of the retail price because typically you will not be making retail sales. Your sales will be at wholesale, sold to third parties who, in turn, sell them to the end user, the customer who listens to the audiobook. We discussed back-of-the-room sales, so you may be personally selling to end users, but that is not typical for most audiobook publishers. If that actually is your main venue, then perhaps a royalty based on retail is fair. On the other hand, if you are doing back-of-the-room, sales you are most likely selling your own writing and narration, so there will be no royalty issue, unless you had to license your work back from a third party.

Your wholesale price will vary, depending upon the customer. If you use a distributor for sales, then your audiobook will be sold at whatever wholesale rates that company has negotiated with the various retailers and wholesalers, and your royalty will be calculated on monies you are paid by your distributor for sales of your audiobooks. For example, if your distributor sends you a check for $100, your royalty is based on that. (Oops, I mean sends you payment via ACH, Venmo, or whatever electronic payment methods are in place when you are reading this guidebook.) Your payment from the distributor is net after the distributor has taken their percentage.

You want your outgoing royalties to be based on *net sales*. Add a definition of net sales to your contract so that you and the licensor are on the same page, so to speak, about how monies due to them are to be calculated.

In royalty accountings, just as with calculating income taxes, *net* means the amount of gross revenue after allowing for subtraction of specific costs. With audiobook accounting, *net sales* means revenue received minus sales tax or shipping costs. The point of this definition is to ensure that you aren't paying royalties on anything other than actual sales revenue. It does not, however, give you license to deduct your costs of producing the audiobook, such as narrator fees, studio costs, or manufacturing, to name a few. It does mean you are not paying royalties on monies that your distributor took as their fee. That is why the phrase *monies received* is important. It is also important because you may have shipped goods, if dealing with hard copy, but not been paid for them. Until those invoices are paid, that account receivable is not money received. In short, you are not calculating royalties on theoretical revenue but on actual payments. Similarly, if a download site sends you a statement showing sales, but you have not yet received payment from them, neither are those considered in calculating monies received.

If the other party insists on having the royalty based on the retail price, then try to get them to agree to a royalty rate reduced by half. Instead of 10 percent, for example, the royalty will be 5 percent. The reason for this is that wholesale prices tend to be in the vicinity of 40 to 55 percent, so 5 percent of retail sales will be roughly equivalent to 10 percent of wholesale sales.

It can be a bit confusing. Here's an example. Your audiobook will retail for ten dollars. You offer a royalty of 10 percent of net revenue, often called net income. That per unit wholesale price will be roughly four or five dollars per unit sold. Ten percent of five dollars per unit is fifty cents per unit. The agent balks and insists on a royalty of 10 percent of the suggested retail price. The response to this is you can offer a royalty on the retail price, but the royalty rate has to come down. Half of the 10 percent royalty, which is 5 percent (I know, I'm the master of the obvious), means you are going to be calculating a royalty of fifty cents per unit, because 5 percent of ten dollars, the retail price, is fifty cents.

Do you see how those amounts are equivalent?

You may end up having to agree to a royalty based on the retail price, though, if the other side plays hardball. That may take you back to your calculator to determine whether this is a cost-effective project for you to undertake. It is possible that there is still wiggle room between your desired wholesale royalty rate and their desired retail rate. Maybe they will settle at 7.5 percent. There are many possible configurations.

Best-Seller Bonus

Instead of or in addition to escalating royalties, you may be asked to provide a best-seller list bonus. The rationale behind this is that if the book makes a best-seller list, it becomes more visible and when it becomes more visible, the audiobook will benefit from that visibility and so you should pay for that.

While best-seller bonuses are not uncommon in book contracts, they are not as common in audiobook contracts, and I suggest avoiding them when possible. Even absent a best-seller bonus, if the audiobook sells well, the rightsholder will be compensated commensurately by earning out the advance and getting into royalty territory. Recall that this is dependent on what your advance and royalty rates are. If your advance was overly ambitious, the advance may never earn out and never see royalties. If the book does spectacularly well, then royalties are very likely to be due.

If you do agree to a best-seller bonus, keep it as small as possible, and do try to limit the best-seller bonus to *The New York Times* best-seller list, positions one through ten. Otherwise, if the book hits any best-seller list, and there are a great many, the bonus clause may be triggered and you find yourself on the hook for additional monies. Unlike the advance, a bonus is not usually recoupable. Don't let a best-seller bonus request sour you on your deal unless the requested bonus is unreasonably large. What is unreasonably large? It's kind of like what the Supreme Court said of pornography: You may not be able to define it, but you know it when you see it. If you and the rightsholder are at odds over a best-seller bonus, ask to make it recoupable. That may make it more palatable to you and may enable them to secure the clause they are seeking.

You do get bragging rights when you have an audiobook that is successful or is based on underlying material that is successful. The best-seller list does not always move the needle much for audiobook sales, although with a long run on the list or a blockbuster book or movie contemporaneous with your publishing schedule, it may. I suggest that you try to have language specifying that the best-seller bonus is triggered after a certain number of weeks on the list, and suggest that number is higher than one or two. One or two weeks on the best-seller list is nice but probably not commercially significant for your audiobook.

Reserve Against Returns

Your contract should provide for a *reserve against returns*. This is most important for a publisher selling physical copies, because physical copies have higher returns than digital-only audiobooks, although even digital-only goods can have returns.

The reserve against returns means that if you are paying royalties, you can hold back some of the royalty money in the event of future returns. This is not a holdback of any advance monies, just royalties. The idea is to ensure you don't overpay. For instance, let's say you sell $20,000 worth of audiobooks. If your contract had a

$1,000 advance and a 10 percent royalty, you would now owe the rightsholder another $1,000. The first $1,000 earned out at $10,000 of sales because 10 percent, the royalty rate, of $10,000, the amount of sales, equals $1,000, the amount you paid as an advance. That leaves the next $10,000 subject to royalty calculations.

Now let's suppose $1,000 worth of returns come back to you. Instead of having sold $20,000 of audiobooks, it turns out you have sold $19,000 worth. The royalty due should have been $900, not the $1,000 you paid.

But you thought ahead: Your reserve against returns clause allowed you to hold back 25 percent of the royalties. That means you actually sent out a check for $750, not $1,000. *Whew!* You are not upside down with the rightsholder after all.

Reserves against returns should have a provision that any monies not actually allocated against returns will be paid to the author in a subsequent accounting period. Some rightsholders will want this to be just one accounting period later, but a fuller picture of sales, in my view, suggests holding the reserve for two accounting periods. That means that if in January you paid a royalty and withheld a reserve against returns, you will not return it in July, but rather in the following January, on the accounting statement due at that time. Meanwhile, by the way, you can take a reserve against returns in the July accounting period too, and that reserve will also be returned, if not used, or to the extent not used, two accounting periods subsequent.

Some rightsholders will want the reserve provision to terminate after a year or two. One year is too soon. If you must cap your ability to have a reserve against returns, agree to terminate that provision after two years, which will be after the fourth accounting statement has been generated. To be clear, this isn't a time period that runs from the date of the contract or from first publication of the audiobook. This has to do with the number of accounting periods.

Notice Provision

A contract should have a notice provision. This is where both parties list the address and name of the person to contact in the event you need to send notice. Let's say you believe the licensor has breached the agreement by permitting another audio publisher to come out with an audiobook based on the same materials you have licensed on an exclusive basis. The notice provision tells you to whom and at what address to send notice of breach of the contract and start the *cure period*, if there is a cure period. Similarly, if you are late with accounting statements, the rightsholder will know to what address and to whom to send the notice of breach based on failure to timely account.

A *cure period* is the time during which someone in breach of the contract has to fix the issue. If the fix is within the cure period, the contract continues, unchanged. If not, the contract should provide what the affected party's remedies are, whether that means to consider the contract terminated or some other form of redress. The redress options should also be specified in the agreement.

Often the notice clause will dictate the agreed methods of delivering notice, whether by mail, email, or overnight carriers such as FedEx. This is so that you don't later disagree about whether the delivery method was appropriate, meaning the notice was properly provided.

There are other reasons to give notice, such as a change of address. Giving notice isn't just for serving notice of breach.

BREACH OF CONTRACT

This brings us to the question of what constitutes a breach of contract. Breach of contract essentially means a party to the agreement did not do what they were required to do under the terms of the contract. In a well-drawn agreement, there may be specifically identified events that can give rise to a breach of contract and trigger a reversion or termination. In the absence of specifying what constitutes a breach, you can notify the licensor that they are in breach, or they may notify you that you are in breach if any substantive part of the contract is not being correctly performed in a timely manner. I prefer the document to be specific as to what constitutes the type of breach that can give rise to the end of the agreement.

Indemnification

You will often find indemnification clauses in any contract, not only in publishing deals. If you are on the receiving end of the contract, you will usually find a clause requiring you to indemnify the licensor in the event of a claim brought against them because of your audiobook. You want to try to limit the language in this clause to any claims brought because of anything you have done in the audiobook that changes, whether by addition or deletion, the underlying work.

This is important. If your audiobook didn't change anything in the book and someone sues based on the content of the audiobook, that isn't something you should necessarily be responsible for. The content was provided to you by the other party to the agreement. Any indemnification clause should be mutual. Mutual clauses mean they apply equally to each party. So, if they provided you with material that gives rise to a lawsuit against you, they will be liable for the costs and fees. It is a two-way street. They want you to protect them from anything you did that gives rise to a claim, and you want them to protect you from anything they did that gives rise to a claim.

It is not usually difficult to adapt the indemnification clause to make it mutual, if it wasn't already written that way.

Occasionally I have been able to change the indemnification clause to cover only *successful* claims by a third party. After all, anyone can bring a claim against you or against the publisher. Someone can say the book is libelous or that your audiobook contained something egregious that injured their ability to earn a living, damaged their reputation, or harmed them some other way. Someone may assert that he is the true rightsholder and you and the licensor are infringing his copyright. If true, then perhaps that person has a good claim, and he should be compensated, or perhaps your audiobook should be withdrawn from the market.

But what if they are unsuccessful in their claim? They have stressed you out, cost you money, and caused you to lose sleep. Should you have to reimburse the publisher for costs of a spurious claim? It doesn't hurt to try to change the typical language of indemnification of any and all claims by adding the word *sustained* or *successful* to the word *claim*. Sometimes this language will be accepted but often the publisher will not agree to it.

Assignment

Most contracts have an assignment clause. What that means is you either can or cannot assign, i.e. sign over, your rights to another person or an entity. Some contracts will say you cannot assign your rights without the written consent of the other party. In a licensing agreement, I find this is fair. The licensor has made an arrangement with you, whether you are an individual or a corporate entity. They have decided to entrust rights to you based on whatever it is that convinced them to say yes, whether it was money, your marketing ideas, or your reputation. If you, in turn, could assign those rights to a third party, it may be someone with whom the rightsholder would not want to do business. They are protecting their business decisions, and I cannot find fault with that.

On the flip side, you will have relatively little right to say that the rightsholder cannot assign the agreement because they stand in a different situation than you do. In essence, what they can assign is the right to collect money and/or a transfer of ownership of the book and its licenses or unlicensed subsidiary rights. What you may be able to do is structure the clause to limit the ways in which they can assign the contract. The language could suggest they can assign the agreement, and this likely will not require your consent, in the event another person or entity acquires all or most of the assets of the licensor.

I don't want you to think there is never a mutual assignment clause. Often the clause is a short sentence that says something akin to this: "Neither party to this Agreement may assign its rights hereunder without the written consent of the other party." It may also say, "such consent not to be unreasonably withheld." Or, to the contrary, it may read: "Either party to this Agreement may assign its rights hereunder." In that case, you are set because if you want to turn your rights over to someone else, you may freely do so.

There is not only one type of assignment clause; these examples are to give you an idea of the flavors they come in.

Venue/Jurisdiction

This is another clause that is not specific to publishing. A paragraph that specifies the venue or jurisdiction in which a dispute is to be brought is standard in most contracts in any industry. Sometimes deals go south, sometimes misunderstandings lead to mediation, arbitration, or a lawsuit. When that happens, if the contract states where such actions are to be brought and under which state's laws, then both parties can evaluate whether bringing a claim is worthwhile, based on the cost and the likely result under the designated state's laws.

The party with the most "juice" will be the one who will choose the jurisdiction and controlling laws. The party with the most juice is the one who has the upper hand in the relationship. Did you license from one of the major New York publishers? You can count on the contract stating any claim will be brought in New York and adjudicated under New York law. If you live in California, that is not convenient for you, but you will likely be unable to change that clause.

Accounting Statements

Your contract will require that you provide sales accountings and payments, if due, on a regular basis. That timetable will be in the contract. A typical calendar provides for statements to be sent twice a year. As with everything else, this is typical but need not be sacrosanct. You might agree to annual, quarterly, or even monthly reports. So long as you are able to do what you are agreeing to do, the timetable is flexible. If it is not feasible, let the other party know. If, for example, your accounting software is set up to report on a quarterly basis, you may accidentally breach the accounting clause for a title to which you agreed to report monthly. My view is that if reports are sent on the same schedule, all of the publishing contracts for your company should reflect that same schedule. If, however, you feel confident that your accounting department can handle the anomaly, you can agree to any timetable you find palatable.

Make sure you keep track of when statements are due and, as important, make sure you do not spend the money that belongs to your licensor and not to you. Whenever you are paid for sales, put the licensor's portion safely away in a bank account specifically for the purpose of paying royalties. This way, when it is time to prepare and send an accounting statement and payments, you are not struggling to do so. At a minimum, keep strict accounting books so if the monies are commingled with your company's other funds, you have a clear line item or items that indicate how much of that money is for royalties. This should be a deterrent to spending those monies, whether inadvertently or otherwise.

This may sound like common sense and it is, but not every person or company remembers or has the willpower to do this. Make it a no-brainer. Make sure you never touch the money that does not belong to you. If you already have the hang of being a steward for royalty money and you wish to keep it in your company's operating account, that's fine. Wherever it is, safeguard it.

Be sure to keep copies of every accounting statement you prepare; it is essential that your checkbook or other method of payment is also kept up to date. Your contract will almost certainly have an audit clause, and if your accounting books are a mess, an audit will be embarrassing at best and possibly costly to you.

An audit clause gives the licensor the right to examine your accounting records to see whether the statements you have sent are accurate. Most contracts limit the exercise of this right to once every twelve months and usually are restricted in scope to the previous two years of statements. Some contracts require a Certified Public Accountant to do the audit, and some do not. Many provide that if the audit turns up discrepancies in excess of 5 percent in the licensor's favor, you will have to pay the costs of the audit, as well as make immediate payment of monies past due.

NARRATOR CONTRACT

Also included at the back of this book are two contracts to use in hiring a narrator for your audiobook. They cover the same basics, but you may prefer one over the other. Know that these, too, are just skeletons of a narrator contract, and there are many varieties. You will come across others in your career. They do not have to look the same so long as they cover the necessary clauses and do not include any unnecessary ones that you can't stomach.

Let's analyze the first contract, but before we do I want to caution you to never have more than one narrator offer out at a time, unless you are seeking multiple narrators. The reason is that if more than one comes back with yes, you are in a pickle. That's not all. It is possible the two narrators' agents know each other and may learn the same offer is out to both actors, which can leave you high and dry. This may sound implausible, but it happened to me. On behalf of a publisher, I had made an offer for a high-profile actor to narrate a terrific book. The publisher was impatient and insisted I make a second offer to another actor while we awaited word on the first. I phoned the actor's manager who listened to the description of the project and the offer, put his hand over the phone and yelled to his partner, "Hey, don't we have an offer for this project for our other client?" Yup. We had not known both actors had the same representation. Egg on face. Neither actor took the gig and a cautionary tale was born.

Now, let's look at a narrator contract clause by clause. It is much shorter than your licensing agreement, so it won't take long to go through.

The very first thing is the title of the contract. It is called the Narration Agreement, but it could be called Narrator's Agreement, Voice Talent Agreement, or any other similar name. I suppose you could call it anything you want, even something unrelated to audiobook recording, but that might make it a little difficult to find on your hard drive.

In the opening language, which is the unnumbered paragraph between the contract's title and the first numbered paragraph, there is some introductory language. You have probably seen this before in other contracts. It just names the parties to the contract. Often it will include their addresses, but sometimes you will find the addresses under the signature lines instead of or in addition to here.

Another thing in that opening language is that I have called you the Publisher, but I have put the word Producer in parentheses. This is not because you need both words. You do not. It is an adaptable agreement so that if the contract is directly with the publisher, you will use *Publisher* to identify the person or entity hiring the voice talent. If it is a producer engaging the narrator, then get rid of the word *Publisher* and use *Producer* instead. It all depends on the circumstances of the project.

The first numbered paragraph is straightforward. It sets forth that the narrator will record the particular project, and here you can put the name of the project. You could name the project in the title of the contract as well, if you wish. The point is to have some specificity so that both the publisher and the narrator, and anyone else who may view the agreement, know they are talking about the same project. It also may include the date by which the narrator is expected to conclude recording and to deliver the audio files. If the narrator is working from a home studio without a director, the contract should also include what she is expected to deliver to you: unedited or edited audio files? In what format, e.g. WAV files, other files? You may also include the specific manner in which the files are to be delivered, such as a private FTP site or by such sites as WeTransfer.com or Box.com, and to whom she should send the audio files. On the other hand, you also could state that the parties agree to deliver the files according to the publisher's requirements, which are to be provided to the narrator, rather than including them in the contract itself.

Numbered paragraph two states what the narrator will be paid for his work on your project.

Paragraph number three specifies that all rights to the resulting recording belong to the publisher or producer. If the contract is between the producer and the talent, rather than the publisher and the talent, make sure, as publisher, that the producer assigns any and all rights, including copyright, over to your company, or to you as an individual in the event you are publishing without using some form of business entity. As to whether you should publish without forming a business, please look at Chapter 10 for my take on the answer to that question. A quick preview: No, you should not.

The fourth paragraph states that the narrator assigns all of their rights in the recording, if any, to you. This assignment is important because copyright law provides for only specific instances of Works for Hire, so even if you use those magic words, Work for Hire, the contract will not make it one if it doesn't qualify under the law. Similarly, a short document called Assignment of Copyright is a protection that can be filed with the Copyright Office. I recommend this document accompany your contracts to your narrators, producers, and directors. If you have original art prepared for the cover, it isn't a bad idea to get an Assignment of Copyright from the designer, as well. He may balk, as copyright to art is something that tends to favor the artists, but if the designer is willing to do this, it gives you ownership of the art. If the designer will not assign the copyright to you, make sure your agreement with him is in writing and allows you to use the art not just for the cover of your audiobook but also in advertising, promotion, and any other ways relevant to its use in regard to your audiobook and your company. Make sure it includes language permitting you to credit the artist. Odds are the artist will appreciate that clause.

While we are on the topic of licensing cover art, many artists' agreements limit usage of the image by both number of copies and a term of years. If you can afford to do so, think ahead and make the number of copies higher than you expect to sell because if you exceed the agreed number, you can no longer use the image. In the alternative, have the contract provide for a fee to be paid in event you go over the agreed number.

This is tricky with downloadable audio because you aren't selling physical copies, so are the sales including the jpeg? Does that count toward your limit? These are all things to be negotiated, although if the artist or his representative doesn't require a limit, you certainly should not mention it. Not all artists have those restrictions. The point is to be mindful if your agreement limits your use in some way.

Back to the narrator agreement. Paragraph five is simple. It just says the narrator can do the job she is being hired to do. This is essentially a warranty from the narrator to the publisher/producer that she is capable of providing the work and will do so.

Paragraph six gives you, the publisher, permission to use the narrator's picture and biography in publishing and promoting the audiobook. Ask the narrator for a headshot or other photo of their choice. Make sure it is acceptable to you, not just in appearance but that it can be used as needed, on packaging or in promotional materials, and so forth.

Paragraph seven is a little stickier. It purports to restrict the narrator from performing on other recordings of the same audiobook. I have never heard of this paragraph being enforced or challenged, but it is good to know what it means. It may not even matter to you whether your voice talent records the same book for someone else, but it probably should, so there will not be confusion in the marketplace about which version was published by which publisher.

Paragraph eight simply means that if anyone succeeds you or the narrator as a party to this contract, whether by assignment or because you sell your company, or someone inherits it, the new parties to the contract are entitled to the same rights and will have the same liabilities that the original parties have. This is a pretty standard contract term in most types of businesses.

Paragraph nine is also a standard contract term. It says that if one part of the contract is found to be unenforceable, the rest of the contract is still valid. The point of this is to ensure that the contract can continue to be enforced, even if one clause is challenged and the challenge succeeds.

Paragraph ten, also standard, says that nothing outside of the terms of this contract can have any impact on the agreement unless the parties later agree, in writing, to change a part of it. In short, if you and the narrator want to change how this contract works, you need to put it in writing and both parties must sign it. Date it, too, so that it is clearly subsequent to the original agreement.

The last paragraph, eleven, grants the prevailing party the right to seek reasonable attorney's fees if you end up in court over anything in the contract. Variations of this clause may call for mediation or arbitration, rather than the right to sue in a court of law.

That's it. Pretty straightforward, right?

We won't analyze the second narrator agreement as we did the first because the concepts are similar. As with the other sample contracts, make sure to put your information into it, as it is just a template. Notice that where the narrator fee is mentioned, it tells you to choose one manner of payment, either per finished hour or flat fee. Delete the mention of the manner of payment you are not using. If your arrangement includes royalties, add that information in the payment clause.

As I mentioned, someone who prefers to use their own narrator contract may send you one unlike this one, but the meaning of it should be very similar. If it is not, then do not be afraid to ask the other party to explain anything you don't understand.

SUMMARY

Congratulations. You've gone from soup to nuts in contracts in the span of just one chapter. There may be other clauses in licensing agreements that were not covered here, but now you have a handle on the major provisions of an audiobook licensing contract, as well as some of the operating procedures you need to know to run a good shop.

If you do receive a contract with a clause or clauses you do not understand, do not be afraid to ask what they mean. It is better for you if you have your own publishing attorney who can answer questions about unfamiliar contract terms, but if you don't have a publishing attorney, do ask the licensor. Even if you do have a publishing attorney, you may wish to ask the licensor for their interpretation of a clause. Without an explanation, you may sign an agreement without understanding what you, or what you believe they, have agreed to do or not do.

CHAPTER 6

How to Publish

Traditional Audio Publisher,
Self-Publisher, or Hybrid

You have determined to enter the audiobook business or to solidify your presence in it. Now it is time to decide whether to be the audio publisher yourself, to license audio rights you already have to someone else, or even to do some of each, a hybrid of the two. How do you decide what to do?

Let's start with looking at what your resources are. If you do not own any audio rights, then you don't have the option of licensing any to a third party. That makes it easy to know what to do. You will be licensing the rights from someone else and then producing an audiobook.

SELF-PUBLISHING

Or maybe you do own some audio rights to your own or someone else's writings, or you think you do. In that case, as we saw in the earlier discussion on copyright, make sure that you have not given someone else control of the audio rights. Often a book publishing agreement will include audio rights. If you did not exclude them when you signed your book deal, then those rights are not yours to exploit: They are your book publisher's rights to do with as they see fit. On the other hand, your book deal may not have mentioned audio rights at all. In that scenario, those rights did remain with you if the contract states that any rights not specifically granted to the publisher remain with the author; in such case, you are free to produce the audiobook yourself or license the rights to a third party. If the contract doesn't specifically mention audio rights or state that all rights not mentioned stay with the author, but instead claims all rights to the book, including all subsidiary rights, you may need to extricate your audio rights from that publisher.

REVERTING RIGHTS

If you did, inadvertently or otherwise, grant the audio rights to your book publisher, but they are not exploiting those rights and have no intention of doing so, ask them (nicely, remember?) to revert the rights to you so that you can steward an audiobook to market. The publisher does not have to say yes, but they may very well do so.

I have had more than one client come to me for help in getting all of their rights reverted, not just the audio rights. This is another possibility, especially in the event that the publisher is not abiding by the contract, including failure to send accounting reports on a timely basis or at all, an unpaid advance, or any other lapse. There is the possibility that a publishing attorney can look at your contract and see if, within the letter of the agreement, the interpretation of the rights clause or reversion is in your favor without the need to do anything more. Don't expect a resolution of your matter to be identical to the resolution of someone else's similar situation. Each case is different. My advice is to be realistic but hopeful.

On the other hand, I have also had prospective clients ask me to extricate them from publishing contracts that had not been breached. They just didn't want to be bound by the agreement anymore. That is not a good reason to try to exit a contract. It might be enough to get you out of it, though, if the publisher also wishes to end the contractual relationship. In a situation such as this, were

I your attorney, I might ask the publisher to release you but I would not claim there is any contractual reason for it.

When you publish a book you wrote, whether in audio, e-book, or print, you are a self-publisher. This is true even if you give your company a name other than your name. Pretty Good Publisher, Inc. is still a self-publisher if the only works you publish are your own. There is nothing wrong with this. We are just defining the type of publisher you are.

TRADITIONAL PUBLISHER

What if your plans are bigger than just one or two audiobooks? You intend to become a full-fledged audio publisher, with a regular schedule of audiobook releases. Why not? There is much material available to continually feed a publishing program. You can publish audiobooks based on rights you already have, or you may learn of books which feel right for your line and are already published or in the pipeline at other publishing houses. New books are written every day. There are plenty of audio rights awaiting a good home.

HYBRID PUBLISHING

The hybrid model, which is a descriptive term I am using and not necessarily used in the industry, is when a company both publishes audiobooks and also licenses audio rights it controls to third parties. There may be a number of reasons to sublicense rights to books they choose not to produce as audiobooks. This happens with the major publishers, as well as smaller houses, who dig deep into their rights to publish numerous audiobooks but still control audio rights to many other works they do not plan to bring out in audio format. In fact, a good resource for you as an audio publisher is to ask the subsidiary rights department at each of the major houses, and any other publishers whose lists are of interest to you as a possible resource, to put you on their list for the rights guide (defined below) for each season. You can be inundated with opportunity if you wish, since many imprints at the major houses have their own subsidiary rights lists. If you get in touch with each imprint and ask to be placed on their list, you will be getting more than one rights guide per publishing group.

RIGHTS GUIDES

What is a rights guide? It is a publisher's list of upcoming books, by title, author, fiction or nonfiction, and a précis of the content; it sets out the rights available for each one. It often will list the author's previous books, if any. You may notice some lists have upcoming books that are intriguing to you. The rights guide makes it easy to find out whether audio rights to each are available and, importantly, who to contact to inquire about them, whether it is the publisher or an agent. These guides are usually available well in advance of the season they cover.

Subsidiary rights departments might send you a list in July of books planned for the following spring. That is how many publishers work, planning their publication lists many months in advance of publication date. If you intend to publish hard copy for distribution to bookstores, you too will want to prepare your seasonal publishing lists well in advance of publication date because the buyers at bookstores have a budget for the season. If your titles are presented late, after the buyer has spent his budget, you will have a tough time getting stores to take in your products. The usual caveats apply here: If the project is exceptionally high profile, you may be given a commitment from bookstores to order copies, even if the season's purchasing has already been completed.

If you have a distributor, they will have a closing date for their own catalog. If you want them to offer your upcoming publications to the retail market, you will need to get them the information they require for each title so that they can present your publishing list to the store buyers. They will let you know what information they need in order to have your titles showcased in whatever season they are cataloging. They will have deadlines, which tend to be hard deadlines. There may be a little wiggle room. This is not a bad thing because it will teach you, as a publisher, to have discipline in learning to have a publishing schedule yourself.

SUMMARY

This short chapter introduced you to the different types of audiobook publishers and explained rights guides to you. One last word on that topic: You can start out as one type of publisher and find that you prefer to be a different type. You might first be a self-publisher and then realize you have rights to sell, too. You might want to start looking at other publisher's rights guides to branch out into publishing other writers. Maybe some people you know have asked you to turn their book into an audiobook. Don't feel constrained to wear a label. These explanations simply lay a foundation for the various ways to find underlying material.

CHAPTER 7

What Makes an Audiobook Sound Good?

Narrators, Studios, and Engineers—Oh My!

HIRING YOUR NARRATOR

If you already know who will be recording the book for you, cross that off of your to-do list. Most often, audio producers have to think about matching the right vocal talent to the book. This includes thinking about factors such as the ages of the main characters, whether the book is best read by someone with expertise in the subject, whether you need more than one narrator, and whether gender or heritage is germane to the casting decision.

Celebrity Narrators

When is it okay to want to hire a celebrity to narrate? Anytime, really—simply because she will add a recognizable name to the project. But don't hire just any celebrity. Consider whether the person you are courting can enhance your project. Is the celebrity related in some way to the subject of the book? Or do you just think it would be a good idea for no reason other than her fame? Put her on your wish list, but as you likely surmise, a yes from a celebrity will increase your costs. Most do not work for a per finished hour fee. Their agent will want a sizable sum, and if you are an unknown quantity to them, they may ask for payment even before the recordings have begun. Do try to get payment to follow the conclusion of the gig rather than its commencement so that your actor has an incentive to show up—and so that if it turns out she is unable to do the work for any reason, you do not have to try to get your money back.

If the celebrity does have a significant and meaningful connection to the project, you may be able to get him for a reasonable fee. An example of this might be that the celebrity has optioned the film rights so you know he is interested in the material, or maybe he grew up in the area profiled in the book. There are many reasons a person may have an interest in something that would otherwise bring a flat no.

Non-Celebrity Narrators

Non-celebrity narrators can be found in a number of ways. If you have a good idea of some talent that will be a good match for the book, come up with your short list of prospective narrators. You may already know your narrator; in some cases, it may even be the author.

Should the Author Narrate?

How can you determine whether and when the author should narrate his own book? This is a little bit of a hot button issue. Some producers strongly believe the answer is never, or nearly never. Some are agnostic on the point. My belief is the author should narrate a nonfiction book when it is within her area of expertise and her narration would help the authenticity of the project. What I mean is if an expert in a field writes a book, it may be full of nuance and language that is difficult for a non-expert to deliver appropriately. Inflections and pronunciations may be incorrect and that rubs some of the sheen of expertise off of it. On the other hand, if the author expert narrates, then even if she speaks with a dull monotone or stumbles a lot—although we hope not so much that the editor can't fix it—she may still be the right person to narrate. Such a dull narration might not be beneficial, though, and perhaps the author in such a case should not be the voice for the audio after all. It's not always an easy decision. Sometimes the author will insist and that makes the decision for you.

Easier, though, is choosing whether the author should narrate fiction. I am not in favor of that, unless the author has exceptional skills. A good example of an author with these skills is Neil Gaiman. He is an extraordinary narrator and brings his own work to life beautifully.

There are a few reasons I don't always prefer author narrators. Interestingly, although you would think the author would know the cadence and rhythm of their own work and so be the best person to read the book aloud, I find that author narrators often don't give correct intention, or inflection, to sentences. I was greatly surprised by this the first few times it happened, but now I know that it is okay to interrupt the author to ask whether they think the sentence or phrase would sound better read differently, which is my way of saying that I think it would sound better read differently—and then I give them the reading I thought they intended all along. More often than not, the author will agree with me. I wonder if this is partly nerves from being in a setting different than the one where she puts pen to paper or fingers to keyboard. It is also because narrating is very intensive work, as your eyes are on the text at all times, so sometimes it is hard to take in the meaning of a paragraph or sentence, or even a phrase, and to provide the correct delivery, notwithstanding that the author is the person now speaking the very words they wrote.

Another reason not to prefer the author as narrator is that many are simply not very good at reading aloud. They know how to pronounce words (or most words, anyway), but their reading may be flat and dull. That is not an enticement to keep listeners listening. It is not an enticement to getting listeners to leave good reviews, and good reviews can lead to more purchases and more listeners. I have a high tolerance for less-than-stellar narration when listening to an audiobook, but I can recall at least one best-selling book to which I could not listen because the author's narration was so dull.

Yet as I've said, even a dull author narrator is a good choice when the book is a subject within their particular expertise, whether that is a scientific or mathematical tome or a memoir.

The point is simply not to have the author be your default narrator. Put thought into the question of who to use as voice talent. A good choice of reader is a vital part of what makes a good audiobook good.

How Do You Choose Your Narrator?

So, you've determined that both a celebrity and author narrator are off the table. How do you find a narrator, otherwise?

If you are someone who listens to audiobooks, you may have some favorite narrators already. Are any of them an appropriate voice for your project?

If you don't know whom you want to have narrate, listen to some samples. I recommend going to Audible.com or any other audiobook download site and searching for some titles in the same genre as the one you are currently wishing to cast. Each title on Audible has an audio sample, a few minutes of the program you can listen to for free. You will likely find some prospective narrators there. Make a note of their names and the title they read, so that you can easily refer back to the sample, if need be. Once you have your short list of narrators, if you don't already know them, you need to learn how to contact them.

If you do not have contact information for them, try putting their name into a search engine to see whether they have a website.

Most websites include a method for contacting the proprietor or owner of the site, so if you do find their website, look for that information and use their recommended method to send them a query. If you do not find a website for them, try searching for them on Twitter or Facebook or other social media. If your search is successful, send them a message. Be polite and tell them you have a project you would like them to consider.

Another resource I have mentioned more than once in this guidebook is the Audio Publishers Association (APA). Their website address is www.audiopub.org. Make sure you go to dot org because the dot com address is a different website and not related to the APA. It is very possible one or more of your potential narrators is a member. They may have their contact information listed on the APA website.

Another way to find your prospective voice talent is through a voice-over agency. Many agencies have samples of their actors' work available online. If you know the name of the actor you want to use, try to find his agent by using the same methods we have discussed. Use a search engine. When you find him or his representative, make an offer. When you call the agency, you will be asked to send the offer in writing, or their website may tell you that they prefer to receive written offers via email without a phone call. Whatever their protocol is, abide by it. Some of the agencies with which I have worked include Vox (www.vox.com), Innovative Artists (www.iany.com and www.iala.com), Special Artists Agency (www.specialartists.com) and CESD (www.cesdtalent.com).

A wonderful thing about voice-over agencies is that if you work with them a few times, you can establish a good relationship to the point where you can send an email or pick up the phone to tell an agent about your project and see who she recommends. She will take into consideration what you tell her you are seeking in a narrator, but be sure to keep in mind that your goals and the agent's goals are similar but not the same. She wants to procure work for her client; you want to procure the talent of a voice-over artist who is appropriate for your project. She may come up with recommendations you don't think are a good fit. It is okay to say, "No, thank you." It is okay to tell the agent you will think about it, if you are unready to say yes or no to any particular name.

IMDbpro.com is a very good resource. Owned by Amazon .com, IMDbpro.com has a page for most actors working on the large and small screens (film and television) and often has contact information for their representatives. I have found many narrators using IMDbpro. Sometimes the contact will be an agent; sometimes it will be a manager. Sometimes you may be surprised to find that you are contacting the actor directly. At times, there will not be contact information listed at all. Those are the tough ones. IMDbpro.com, unlike its little brother IMDb.com, is a subscription service and the annual fee may be money well spent, depending on how often you think you will use it. I subscribe to it and find it well worth the money. If you don't want to subscribe, you can also try using a search engine with the actor's name and the word *agent* and see what comes up.

IMDbpro.com will often have multiple contact listings for actors. When you see a listing for a voice-over agent, try that company or person first. Even if the actor is also represented by an agency for film, television, or stage, if you go to those agents first, they will likely refer you to the voice-over agent anyway. This is not always the case, but since you are seeking their services for voice-over, the voice-over agent is the logical place to start. If you don't get a reply from that contact, then move on to another one, whether a publicist or another agent, if these alternatives are shown on the actor's IMDbpro.com page.

One more technique I have used comes in handy when none of your resources turn up contact information for your desired narrator. This technique is particularly successful for well-known actors. A handful of top agencies and management companies in the United States tend to represent most, albeit not all, of the top-grossing actors. If the person you seek is a household name, call each of the agencies, in turn, to ask whether they represent him. The ones I am thinking of include CAA (Creative Artists Agency), WME (William Morris Endeavor), ICM Partners, UTA (United Talent Agency), Paradigm Talent Agency, APA (Agency for the Performing Arts), The Gersh Agency, and LBI Entertainment. Sometimes you learn that one of these agencies does indeed represent the talent you are looking for, and then you can move forward with making an offer for his services.

Where Should Your Narrator Be Located?

Since narrators can be anywhere in the world and still record your book, they don't need to be local to you. If you do want local talent, search for voice-over agents in your area and inquire whether they have clients who have narrated audiobooks. Ask for samples. Don't be afraid to listen to some of what the talent can do. This person is going to be working with you to create something, so it behooves you to do some research to ensure the talent seems right for your project.

How to Make an Offer

When reaching out to someone, make sure to give pertinent information. The book is called such-and-such by author so-and-so. Briefly describe what the book is about. Tell her the likely running time and how long you think will be needed in the studio. What is your time frame for recording? That is important information so that a narrator knows whether or not she can meet your deadline.

Make an offer for the narrator's work, either based on a per finished hour rate or a flat fee if you prefer (see Chapter 3 for details), or any other yardstick. Don't ask a narrator to work for free unless you know the person very well and she or he has a deep interest in helping you bring your audiobook to life.

The exception to this guideline, perhaps, is using a narrator you find via ACX, the Audible-owned site for matching projects with narrators, or through services similar to that of ACX, such as Findaway Voices (findawayvoices.com). As of this writing, one option on ACX is for a narrator to agree to forego an up-front fee in exchange for a percentage of the revenue from sales of the audiobook. So, this is not really asking a narrator to work for free, as I had intimated. It is asking the narrator to defer compensation until revenue is received. At that time, they will receive an agreed-upon portion of that revenue.

Anecdotally, a royalty share arrangement without any advance is more popular with newer narrators than those with experience because many audiobooks earn little money. Experienced narrators who agree to such arrangements often find they actually were working for free or very little compensation. Still, you may attract an experienced narrator if there is something about your book that is particularly enticing or suggests a good cash flow once it is available for sale.

MULTI-VOICE PRODUCTIONS

When to Use More Than One Voice

Sometimes audiobooks have more than one narrator. You need to consider whether multiple voices are an enhancement to your recording. A nonexhaustive list of when to use more than one performer includes the following.

- Chapters are told in the first person from more than one point of view; so, by way of example, you may have a male narrator in the first person and a female narrator in the first person. For this, two narrators will better serve your program than one voice that handles both points of view, or POV, as it is often called for short. In the case of multiple POVs, you may want to ask one male and one female actor to vary their voices to signify the different personalities for each gender, rather than hire a different narrator to voice each part.
- Some books have chapters in first person and other chapters in the third person. This can be done with one narrator, or it may be a case where two narrators better suit the material.
- Your project is akin to a radio drama or a reading of a play, calling for multiple voices because there are multiple parts, which may or may not interact.
- There are portions of the book which are told in voices different than that of the protagonist or main storyteller, such as a nonfiction book by a doctor who includes quotes from patients. This doesn't require using a second voice; it is a choice for the publisher or producer as to whether it will better serve the material or act as a distraction.

JESSICA'S FOURTH RULE FOR AUDIOBOOK PUBLISHERS

What a great place to advise you of yet another of my useful rules! This is true for every audiobook: *Avoid anything that diverts the listener's attention.*

How I determine whether something helps or hinders an audiobook is whether I think it will distract the listener from the book's content. A good example of this is how to pronounce words that have multiple acceptable pronunciations. If one pronunciation has an everyday sound and the other sounds pretentious, go with the everyday one. The pretentious one can lead some listeners to think more about the choice of word than about what is happening next in the narration.

Back to Multi-Voice Analysis

None of these examples absolutely require that you use more than one voice. There are countless audiobooks on the market that have differing POVs but use one talented narrator who has altered his voice to represent each first-person character. This is the same technique many narrators use even in a book written entirely in the third person, in order to differentiate characters. Use your best judgment as to whether it will be a better program with one voice or more than one. If you hire a producer and/or a director, consult with them. They have the necessary expertise to advise you about this issue.

ENGINEERS: WHAT DO THEY DO?

I have directed hundreds of audiobook recordings and worked with hundreds of narrators, but one thing I have not done is learn anything more than a small fraction of what engineers know about the equipment in a recording studio. A good engineer will know the fine points of how to set up the booth, microphone, and attendant electronic equipment, and will be able to troubleshoot the technical aspect of a studio recording. To make a good audiobook, you need to be aware of both what you do know how to do and what you do not know how to do. For example, I know what sounds good and what doesn't, I know what to listen for and how to direct the talent, I know how to operate the recording software Pro Tools on at least a basic level, *but* I don't know the same things someone with technical expertise knows. I would not know which microphone sounds best for a young soprano female versus the microphone for a deep-voiced middle-aged man, for example. The idea that two different types of voices might benefit from using different microphones wouldn't have even crossed my mind if I hadn't seen engineers try different microphones for different types of voices. This is the kind of expertise I trust my engineer to possess.

That trust in your engineer can be earned after having worked with someone previously and obtaining good results. At times, trust is based on a referral from a respected peer. Other times, it is faith that the person purporting to know how to set up and run the studio for an audiobook recording does actually know what he is doing.

What Is a Studio?

The equipment is just one part—an essential part—of what you need to ensure the quality of your work. Other pieces of the puzzle include the quietude of the location, the way the room is constructed or baffled—which does not mean *puzzled* but means that baffling—any item put in the space to help exclude outer sound while keeping the interior of the booth sounding clean and clear—has been strategically employed in the setup of the recording space.

My point is that an important part of having an audiobook sound good is recording in a studio that has good sound. This seems obvious and yet many audiobooks are recorded in substandard studios, or not in a studio at all but in someone's home or elsewhere, and consequently have substandard sound quality unless the home recording is made in an appropriate space. Sometimes this can be fixed relatively easily in post production, meaning working on the audio recording after the recording sessions have ended, but sometimes it cannot be fixed. If you are unsure of whether your audiobook sounds good, ask an experienced and impartial person to listen to a few minutes of the program and give you feedback. Make sure to choose someone who will be frank with you.

I have listened to samples of audiobooks that sound as though they were recorded in tin cans; I have heard some that have echoes. Many have extraneous noises: sirens, paper noise, static, chairs moving, throats being cleared, stomach noise, the sound of someone eating or drinking, dogs barking. While all of these noises are occurrences in our daily lives, they don't belong in your audiobook. As with most things, I do have an exception to this rule, but only one: When your recording is of someone who is speaking at a live event, be it a lecture, a panel discussion, an interview, or the like, the extraneous noise is necessarily present. With a studio, it isn't and it shouldn't be.

A studio, by the way, can be a soundproof booth or other similar space in someone's home. When a narrator has set up their living space to adapt some part of it to the requirements of a good recording, then recording at home is, to my mind, a studio, so long as it has the same quality equipment and the same quiet but not deadened sound as any other recording booth. I am not a technician, and this is not a guide for narrators to learn how to best equip their space or rent a studio appropriate for audiobook recording, so there is not going to be a discussion of how to soundproof or how to determine which microphone is best. But it is important that you, the audiobook publisher, are aware of the standards audiobooks must meet in order to be competitive in the marketplace, and it is important that you have more than passing familiarity with what a good audiobook sounds like. This is about the sound quality, not about how good the content is. That is also essential, but it is a different issue.

Extraneous Noise Means Extraneous to the Narrator's Voice

A studio recording should be able to work around noise interruptions that come from outside the booth. You can stop and wait for the siren to pass, the helicopter to fly away, the slamming door to stop reverberating.

Not all of the aural clutter comes from outside the studio walls. It is impressive how sensitive most microphones are. You will hear stomach noises you would never have noticed if not for the microphone picking up every tummy rumble. If stomach noise is too much of an impediment to smooth recording, stop and eat something. Of course, the irony of stomach noise is that the stomach makes noise when it is empty and it makes noise when it is digesting. Still, a very loud tummy in need of food is worth the pause in work. Or maybe your narrator accidentally kicked the music stand their script is on. Wait for it to stop vibrating after being kicked or after placing your script or tablet on it. Those sounds, too, should come out of the recording. Take the line again. Just rerecord it, being mindful of sound before the narrator resumes speaking. Whatever the source of the extraneous sound, narration should stop for its duration so that whomever is editing your program will be able to excise the noise and present you with a clean-sounding recording.

The editor will remove the extraneous sounds as much as possible, leaving behind a good, well-edited recording.

If you are recording in a studio subject to a lot of outside noise, maybe that isn't the best studio for you. Once or twice I have arrived at a studio and found it completely unsuitable for our purposes and had to leave, which is problematic because it means rescheduling the narrator and may even mean recasting or changing the release date of the audiobook. Thankfully, the internet makes it easier to get recommendations, referrals, and reviews. This isn't a foolproof method but it does narrow the odds of booking an inappropriate place. Still, if you have booked a place you find will not work and are unable to cancel it, whether for economic reasons or otherwise, you will just have to make the best of it. Try to record in the interstices between the noises you need to have edited out. If overall the studio sound just isn't good, there may be no way to make the best of it. You could end up having to rerecord. In such an instance, walk away. The money you have to pay for the unused studio time may be less expensive than if you have to completely rerecord or spend extra on postproduction to try to salvage the program.

When I had my audio publishing company, a studio I often worked in would usually assign me their smallest studio. That was fine with me. They charged me a very reduced rate compared to what they charged musicians to record there, and musicians were their primary clientele. Audiobooks are most often recorded by just one voice and the booth in that room was plenty big enough for that. The drawback to this recording room was that it was along a very busy street and necessitated that we paused recording every time a truck rumbled by, an emergency vehicle turned on its siren, or a motorcycle's engine whined. The studio was otherwise very nice, and I worked there dozens of times over the course of many years. The sound quality from that room was good and knowing how to work around the outside sounds made all the difference between a recording cluttered with noises that didn't belong there and a top-notch recording.

By the time you get into the studio, I hope you have listened to a fair number of audiobooks produced by major publishers so your ear can recognize a good-quality recording. Having prepped for your own audio publishing in this way, have the engineer play back a minute or two of the recording for you from time to time to ensure that it sounds good. It may be surprising to you to learn that often the sound you hear as the book is being recorded is different, sometimes very different, from how it sounds when it is played back. Think of this as a system of checks and balances.

A clear and clean recording matters tremendously for several reasons. First, the author's name, likely the narrator's name and you or your company's name, will be on this recording. Your reputation is at stake. If you want to be known as someone who produces good audiobooks, if you want this particular audiobook to sound good, all of your elements must be of good quality. I say this more than once, but it is vitally important to be cognizant that your audiobook is going out into a marketplace where it will compete with programs that have been produced to the highest standards, in studios well equipped for and familiar with the process of recording a spoken-word program, and edited by professionals who know what a well-edited audiobook sounds like, including which noises to leave in and which to leave out.

Those extra noises can be distracting to the listener. You just learned my Fourth Rule for Audiobook Publishers. One of my primary tests as a director for whether or not something is working is whether I find the noise distracting, or have a concern that our future audience may be brought out of the story by a distraction. If one moment you were listening to the tale of the Pied Piper and his enchanting music and the next moment you are hauled back to the present reality by the sound of a garbage truck picking up a trash can, that is not beneficial to you. You've lost the listener's attention to your story.

The director likely has marked a manuscript for the editor with notes that show which takes to use, where interruptions occurred, and anything specific about the narrator that may help the editor. For example, a note that the narrator has a lot of mouth noise (for example, too little saliva, too much saliva, the click of a denture, swallowing while speaking) may alert the editor to keep her ears open for a particular type of distracting sound, and heightens her ability to clean up those sounds. If you are the director, learn to mark the script so that the editor can follow your notes and implement your instructions.

Narrator Noises

Mouth noise can be an issue because you are aiming for a fairly pristine recording. Extraneous noises are not welcome. There are some narrators who have very little mouth noise and others with whom it is audible on every word. A good editor will be able to minimize the noise, but it is unlikely someone will painstakingly go through all the recording sessions to hand delete mouth noise throughout. If you have a narrator with very noticeable mouth noise, be sure to ask your engineer if she thinks it will be a problem for the editor and be sure to ask your editor if he can get rid of most of it. It may be helpful to have green apples and the oxymoronic unsalted saltines, both of which reportedly help to clear up an overly active palate.

If your narrator auditioned for the gig, then you may already have heard his mouth noise when you heard the sample he submitted. If that sample was clean of mouth noise, that's good news because you know the condition is not necessarily chronic. Have him swish some water around in his mouth from time to time. Mouth noise isn't the end of the world, but if the sound can be ameliorated, it should be.

Most of the time, an editor will not ask for additional money to clean up noise. It is part of the gig. Some gigs are easy to edit, some aren't. It tends to even out. If your editor is asking for additional money for an extraordinarily difficult edit, ask what the issues are. Maybe the recording really is so far out of the norm that a price adjustment is fair.

There may be other issues with a narrator that either irk you or make you wonder whether they are problematic. The issue of vocal fry, for example. Vocal fry, a creaky sound in the lower register of a voice—and something I had never heard mentioned until the past few years—is not something that I would ask a narrator to correct unless it is overused or otherwise jarring. If the narrator was good enough to get the gig, it seems unlikely that their vocal fry will be egregious enough to require drastic measures in studio or in postproduction.

Other Narrator Issues

Once in a while, you may choose to or need to fire your narrator. If she is unable to satisfactorily complete the job you have hired her to do, your choices are slim. You can keep her and hope the magic of editing turns your recording into a terrific audiobook, or you can ask her to leave. This is a situation that calls for tremendous tact. A person's feelings are at stake, and if you are not going to pay her, then her livelihood is also at stake. Thankfully, I have only ever had to let one narrator go from a project. He was a successful film actor, trying to read aloud a very serious and topical nonfiction book. As his struggle with the pages grew evident, he told me that he was dyslexic and that his agent didn't even know he was dyslexic. After we worked slowly through a very few pages while rolling the recording for two hours, I suggested that he did not have to suffer through the project. I gave him the choice to tough it out or to call it quits. Making it his choice meant he could leave with his head held high. He had not been fired. He had been given options.

Another question with narrators is their stamina. Think about how difficult it is to use your voice all day, often for several days at a time, without getting hoarse or having your throat tire. This is something you may be unable to measure until you are in the studio. Your narrator has already been told the work hours, so if she is unable to actually put in the number of hours you have allocated, but she is otherwise right for the gig, you may need to add another day or two to the recording schedule. This happens quite rarely, though. Professional narrators know the limitations of their voices and if they cannot work the schedule you propose, they will usually be straightforward and let you know. I have had narrators tell me they can work only three or four hours per day because otherwise their voice wears out and will not be usable the next day. While I prefer a longer workday, because I like to complete the project in fewer days, this kind of upfront honesty helps me to more accurately gauge the time needed for recording sessions.

Scheduling Your Narrator

Before getting to the studio, you and the narrator need to agree on a recording schedule. Sometimes you will just let him know the dates and times, and if he can make those sessions, then he is hired. If he knows he cannot make all of the sessions as scheduled, and tells you that up front, you have the choice to work around his schedule or thank him, explain that you need to record according to the schedule, and find someone else for your audiobook.

The process is simple. You have made contact with the narrator of your choice, you have told him about the audiobook, he expressed interest, and if you haven't already, now you tell him when you plan to record. This is when a professional narrator will check his calendar and let you know whether the schedule works for him or not. If it does, let him know the studio name and address. If you haven't booked a studio yet, you can get back to the talent when you do have that information. If he is working from his home studio, this is not pertinent.

HOW TO CHOOSE A STUDIO
AND WHAT TO ASK FOR

When you need to rent a studio to record your audiobook, there are things the studio needs to know and there are things you need to know to tell them. First, you need a studio that is suitable for recording an audiobook. We have already discussed that you want one without outside noise continually interfering with your work. Many studios that are fine for recording rock music may not be fine for audiobooks. Loud music masks extraneous noise.

Ask others in the industry for referrals. Audiobooks have been recorded in all types of studios and if someone uses one with a good result, she will be happy to recommend it. If you don't have a trusted referral, use today's version of the Yellow Pages and employ a search engine with the words *recording studios* and the geographic area you want. You are likely to turn something up.

Once you have identified suitable studios, ask what their prices are. They will probably give you an hourly rate. Rates in the United States run the gamut. See if you can find out what is average in that area but also have an idea of what you can afford to pay. I have paid as little as $45 per hour for studio time (but not in many years) and as much as $150 per hour. There are studios that charge much more. Someone recently told me that he did not ask about rates at a studio he had booked and was more than a little taken aback to receive a bill for $300 per studio hour. For most audiobooks, more than $125 an hour or so makes a project expensive. After all, this is just for recording, not for editing or mastering. If you need a lower fee than what is quoted, ask if the studio can give you a break. Maybe they can give you a day rate, as opposed to an hourly rate, if you book an entire day or two, or however many you may need.

You also need to know whether the studio rate includes an engineer. It certainly should and it usually will, but be sure to ask.

Some studios provide separate rates: one for both studio and an engineer and one for just the studio alone. It's essential that you and the studio booker are on the same page and that you will have an engineer for the session. Not only does the engineer know how to use the equipment, most have what I call "engineer ears," by which I mean they can hear things that not even experienced directors hear. That second pair of ears comes in very handy in the process of obtaining the clean recording you are aiming for.

Above all, when booking your recording dates, be very clear with the studio that you will be recording an audiobook. You don't want a vast room in which the reader will lose the intimate sound suited to narration. You also don't want a closet in which the narrator will be uncomfortable. Just make sure the room is large enough to accommodate the voice-over talent, but not so large that he or she will sound distant or echoey.

In addition, make sure there is a way for your director to communicate with the narrator while working, usually referred to as a talk-back button. Make sure the studio knows that your director may want to wear headphones. Your talent may want to, also. This doesn't sound like a big deal, but there have been times when the studio was unprepared to provide headphones to either me or the talent, and locating headphones, getting them set up, and making sure they work eats up time. Any sort of setup you have to do after you arrive uses studio time you are paying for.

As with the studio where I recorded alongside a busy street, some studios will give you a break on price if you can record during their least-busy times. If it is a studio catering mostly to rock or hip-hop musicians, daytime is a good bet. Sometimes a smaller room will be less expensive. If the room is good, then in a studio with multiple recording rooms, you probably do not need to be fussy about which room you use so long as you have the same room for the duration of the project. The reason for needing the same room is that different rooms produce different sounds, and you may hear the difference in your recording. This difference may be evident even to someone without engineer ears. If you are recording multiple narrators in more than one studio, this is a given. You must use more than one room. Don't fret. It is integral to that particular project, and a skilled editor will adjust the sounds of each to make the ambient sound as similar as possible.

Perhaps you will hire an experienced producer and director, or perhaps you will take on these roles yourself. We will touch on the basics of what a director does in the next chapter, in case you are not just the publisher but also the director.

SUMMARY

Chapter 7 introduced you to what goes into casting the right narrator, including how to find them and how to make an offer. You learned my Fourth Rule for Audiobook Publishers, which is to avoid anything that diverts the listener's attention or, as I often say, takes the listener out of the audiobook. We looked at multivoice projects, discussed what engineers do, confronted the issue of extraneous noise, and learned to choose a studio. Next up: What happens when you get to the studio and who does what?

CHAPTER 8

Nuts and Bolts

How the Audiobook Sausage Gets Made
(What Actually Happens in Preparing,
Recording, and Editing Your Audiobook)

Here you are, with a book or other source material and your narrator or narrators and a studio you have reserved. There are practical steps you need to take to ensure you are ready for the recording session. Even if you don't plan to be in the studio yourself, I suggest you make yourself familiar with this section because it will be good for you to know what the process entails.

PRODUCER AND DIRECTOR PREP FOR THE STUDIO

What Does a Producer Do?

It is worth your while to know what kind of preparation goes into the pre-studio work of a producer and director. Whether you intend to fill this role yourself or hire others, it is difficult to know whether someone is doing the job well unless you know what the job encompasses.

The producer is someone who puts together the elements that go into the making of the recording. That can include any or all of the following: hiring the studio, casting the right narrator, hiring an editor, and, if necessary, hiring someone to master the edited sound files. The producer also will hire someone to QC (see the next section) the audiobook.

What Is QC?

In the context of audiobooks, QC means someone listens to the edited files with the manuscript in front of him so that he can see whether there were errors in reading, as well as whether there were errors in editing. Editing errors may include inadvertently deleting sentences or paragraphs; it could mean leaving in multiple takes, so that the narrator is heard reading the same line or lines two or more times. It could mean there was a noise that should have been taken out but was left in. Sometimes lines or even paragraphs are accidentally edited into the wrong part of the program. It could be chitchat between the voice talent and the engineer and director. These sorts of things are denoted during the QC process.

Sometimes the QC person will use a clean, unmarked manuscript to follow along while she listens; or she may have a copy of the director's marked manuscript, so she can see whether the director marked any differences between the manuscript and the words spoken while recording, to indicate intentional changes. The director or QC should make a list of things to point out to the producer, so that he is fully apprised of any digressions from the script. This list can include typos, especially if they differ in meaning from what seems more likely to be the intent of the manuscript. A simple example is when the book says "does not" and means "does," or vice versa. QC should notify the producer of any changes to the script made during sessions and the reason for the changes.

Unless the QC person is extremely skilled and familiar with the process, she should mark any and all discrepancies on a document for the producer who, ultimately, will decide which differences are acceptable and which are not. An experienced QC person may see a typo for what it is and not need to report that change on his report. The QC report should include the page number, the time code, and track number of each problem area, so that the producer and editor can listen to it and make appropriate fixes.

QC provides a valuable service. It is akin to a beta slate of listeners. One way to fix errors found during QC is through what is called a second edit. Second edit is just what it sounds like. The editor is given a list of things you want him to fix. Not everything on the list will be editing errors. Most of them probably will not be. If errors cannot be fixed with a tidier edit, the solution is to have the narrator return to the studio to rerecord anything that is needed. That return to the studio is called a "pickup session."

Back to the producer. He will become familiar with the contents of the book. He may not read it if he is going to hire a director, but he will need to know the genre and the general tone of the book in order to hire the appropriate talent for both the director and narrator. For instance, for a humorous novel, one would be unlikely to hire someone who is known for his gravitas, unless the idea is to counterpoint the content with the voice. That can work, actually. Think of Samuel Jackson's spot-on narration of *Go the F*ck to Sleep*. Don't be offended by the title: It is a real book and it was narrated wonderfully by the great Mr. Jackson. The book's humor was highlighted by the seriousness in his voice.

The point is that to hire a narrator, you need to know the type of voice and facility the narrator can bring to the recording and whether it is a match for the material. Similarly, you want a director who has a facility for whatever genre your project falls into. Most directors can easily move from one genre to another, so this is rarely a big issue.

What Does the Director Do?

If you are going to direct, you need to read the book, cover to cover, and preferably before you begin recording. Things a good director does before setting foot in the studio include, to the extent possible, understanding the material so that he can guide the narrator's performance as needed to bring the correct mood and emphasis to the script. An example is the title of the book *Eats, Shoots & Leaves*. The author cleverly titled her book to show how punctuation matters. Does someone eat shoots and leaves of plants? Or does someone eat, shoot—whether dice or something more dangerous—and go away? This is where you may need to help your narrator. If something in the book requires a specific type of enunciation or inflection or emphasis which differs from how she has said it, give them the correction and the reason for it. As an example, a sentence could need emphasis on the word 'day' because it contrasts with 'night' in a previous sentence. Part of the director's job is to ensure that words are spoken in a way that transmits their meaning to the listener, so if someone has given emphasis to the wrong word or, as the joke goes, put em-PHA-sis on the wrong syl-LA-ble, correct them. This isn't preparatory, this is what happens in the studio but it bears mentioning here so that you know what sorts of things you need to be prepared to encounter.

Another reason the director should read the entire book before beginning to record is that there may be something late in the book that influences the manner in which the recording should proceed. I once directed a novel in which it turns out that the main character, whose story is told in the first person, is not a young man as the reader or listener is led to believe, but is a young woman. The producer was very smart to choose a male narrator with a soft voice. But think what could have happened if the director did not know that the protagonist is actually a woman. The information gleaned from reading suggested information about the character that we didn't want to let on to the listener. It was a surprise to the person reading the book the traditional way, so it should also be a surprise to the person "reading" the book with their ears via audiobook.

This is particularly tricky when dealing with a surprise character whose voice is distinctive. Consider this example: A British doctor turns out to be the murderer but until the reveal, the murderer's thoughts are unattributed because the author doesn't want the reader to know who the bad guy is until late in the book. How do you keep the listener from knowing who the killer is when you have to record those thoughts? You don't want to give away the identity by using the same voice used for the character in other scenes. One possibility is electronically altering the voice. Another possibility is to have the thoughts expressed in a whisper or even at normal volume but without the accent. That might be a bit of a cheat, but it keeps the secret intact.

Whatever you decide to do, the point is that you knew the issue was there and you gave thought as to how to handle it.

Reading the entire book will provide clues for the recording. You may learn that a character is Irish. You didn't know that because the setting is North Carolina, and there was no reference early in the book to the character's nationality. If that character has been voiced as a Southerner, their lines came out wrong.

One more example of why it is important to prep: I once directed a novel where a character's name changed halfway through the book. That wasn't a clever ploy of the author, it was a mistake. He had changed the character's name from the first draft to the last draft but the change was not made throughout the manuscript. It would be a tough fix to redo half a book because the character's name was in error.

Yet another reason to read the book before recording is to make what I call a pronunciation list. This is the bane of many directors, but it is also their greatest assistant. This list is words you need to look up so that you can tell the narrator how to pronounce them. It could be words from another language. It could be scientific terms or names, real or imagined. Think how much time you would use up in the studio—time you are paying for—to stop and look up words when they could and should have been researched before the recording started. You, or a researcher if you hire someone to do this work for you, will be very busy looking up foreign words or names or even common English words that may be commonly mispronounced. As a matter of fact, the very word *pronunciation* is often mispronounced as *pronounciation*. The payoff is that your director will enjoy not having to slow down while in the studio other than to feed the correct pronunciation to the narrator. The narrator, too, will be glad not to have to spend time waiting while the director researches something.

You will find yourself putting some ordinary words on the list as well, because there may be words you are sure you know how to pronounce, but you fear won't come to mind when you need them. You may recognize what some of those words are from previous experience, and so you put them on the list. The narrator may blow right past those words with no difficulty, but you will be prepared just in case the same words that sometimes trip you up also stump her. Anything you think may present such a glitch belongs on your pronunciation list, no matter how prosaic the word. Would I be a bit embarrassed if someone looked over my shoulder and saw basic English words on my list? Yes, I would, but I'll take being a little sheepish over being unprepared.

In another scenario, if you are about to embark on recording a fantasy novel, there will likely be all sorts of names of people, places, and animals that the author has made up. It is a great help to have access to the author so that you know how he wants these to be pronounced. If you don't have access to the author, try other ideas. Is this book (or an earlier one in the series) already published and enjoying a fan base? How do the fans say these names? You may be able to find some but not all of the pronunciations. You may find discrepancies in how the words are said. That's a director's life. You work hard, you exhaust your reference materials, and sometimes your best guess is as close as you can come.

There are lots of resources for looking up words. Even when it seems overwhelming, and sometimes it will, you will find much of what you need. The Resources section of this book will give you a head start in finding many of the answers to pronunciation questions.

Once you have your pronunciation list, start looking up how to say each one. Sometimes I look them up after the list is complete, and sometimes I look them up as I go. However you do it, make sure you have your list ready by the time you get to the studio so that you minimize the amount of in-studio time you need to use for anything other than recording. You are probably paying a studio an hourly fee, not per finished hour but actual hours used—or sometimes actual hours booked, even if you are done earlier than you anticipated.

You will often need to look things up while in the studio because even the most astute eye rarely catches everything while prepping for the session. It happens to everyone. But at least your prep will keep to a minimum the number of times you have to do research during your recording time. Just have resources on hand so that you can look things up as you go. If you do not have a handy dictionary or internet connection during the session, make notes of these words or text discrepancies and deal with them when you return to a place with access to the Web or reference books. That way you can do pickups to fix anything that was spoken incorrectly.

A frustrating truth of preparation is that you will not always be able to find all of the words on your list. Do the best you can. Make educated guesses. Try to determine the root of a word, including its root language. If the word is a transliteration of a language that does not use the Roman alphabet, use Wikipedia to look up the word as it appears in the book. If it has the word in its original language, try copying and pasting it into a tool such as Forvo. You may find the word on Forvo in, let's say, Japanese, but the English transliteration is not found there. In other words, be creative.

There are endless numbers of resources. Do you have Farsi words in your book? Try having dinner at a Persian restaurant and ask the waitress (or another employee there) to spend a few minutes with you looking at your word list and helping you with pronunciations. Yes, I did this. Are you looking for the name of a town in Russia but can't find it anywhere, even on a map? The nearest consulate may be able to help you, even via telephone. They may never have heard of it either, but generally consulates are willing to help where they can. A town you have never heard of in Ohio has a town hall or a local library you can contact to ask how to properly say the town's name. Any other local government office or private business can also be of assistance. If you need to know how to say the name of a road, for example, and you find a phone number for a hotel on that road, call the hotel and ask how to pronounce the name of the road. Oh, and even if you think you know how to say a name, you may want to double-check it. Berlin, Ohio, and Berlin, Germany, are not pronounced the same way—and not just because of a German accent or lack thereof.

Richard Brewer, an author, audiobook narrator, director, and producer, says that he keeps a master list of pronunciations. That is a smart idea. Words you have looked up for one project often crop up in another. This is also helpful for sequels, to keep pronunciations consistent from one audiobook to the next.

He also tracks his pronunciations on a spreadsheet. I use the app Notes on my iPad. Lots of people use word processing programs for their lists. Whatever works for you is fine, even pen and paper.

Use your thinking cap. There are plenty more ways to find the information you are seeking. Be careful, though, not to rile anyone. If you are working on an audiobook that is uncomplimentary to someone, calling their office to ask how to say their name may result in a question as to why you want to know. Do you want to stir a hornet's nest by admitting you are about to release an audiobook that does not paint them in a good light? That would be uncomfortable, to say the least, and it may create a problem for the author as well. Do be creative in finding resources, but use them wisely.

Prepping Your Narrator

You want your narrator to be prepared, so send your pronunciation list to her prior to the recording date, if the list is ready before the studio date. Some narrators will incorporate the pronunciations right into their script. The practical effect of this integration is that the narrator will not have to slow down or stop when she comes to the unfamiliar word because the notes are right there in front of her. If the narrator does not have the list ahead of time or has not incorporated it into the script, the director will have the list at hand and when the tricky words appear, he will either be ready to feed the word to the narrator or pause very briefly while locating the word and providing it to her. These things ensure a smooth session.

Make sure your narrator has the manuscript well ahead of the session so that she can also read it and make notes about things pertinent to her performance. That may include the gender and age of any of the speaking characters, any accents the author describes, and a description of every character so that the narrator can think of how to distinguish the voices from each other.

You are also looking for continuity in the book. You may find some anomalies in the text that warrant an explanation from the publisher or the author. Try to get that before you record so that you can explain it or fix it for your narrator. Sometimes you just have to live with something that doesn't make sense to you or the narrator. Sometimes you will take a moment to rant to each other.

Sorry, authors. It doesn't happen with every book, but it does happen. That's normal. Our frustrations in our work are sometimes lessened by letting off a little steam.

Often a good working relationship will develop between the narrator and the director, and they may end up telling each other personal stories that have been prompted by something in the book, or even something that has nothing to do with the book. This is a good time to stop recording because the stories may be frank and personal, and they are nothing that should be committed to the hard drive of the computer. Stopping the recording is a courtesy. Many times during conversations, narrators have paused and asked whether we were recording. As soon as I know we are veering off into unscripted territory, I will stop recording. The big caveat here is that you must remember to turn the recording equipment back on when the chat is done and work resumes. You do not need to stop rolling if you are just chatting briefly and the conversation is not personal.

In the studio, the recording booth should be set up for the reader, usually with a music stand to hold the script or tablet with the script loaded onto it and ready at the first page he will be reading. Make sure the reader has water at hand and anything else he wants, such as tea or coffee. A popular tea for narrators is Throat Coat. You may want to have black tea, green tea, and chamomile on hand, to offer choices. If you have an experienced narrator, they already know what they need.

What the Narrator Reads and in What Order

The first thing I have a narrator record is what we call the Intro/Outro. This has the introductory and concluding material that starts and ends most audiobooks. Here is an example of an introduction, or intro.

BEST AUDIOBOOK PUBLISHER, INCORPORATED PRESENTS:

> The Best Audiobook Ever, by Master Author
> Read for you by Susie Narrator.

And now, here is an example of an outro.

> This is Susie Narrator. We hope you have enjoyed this production of The Best Audiobook Ever, by Master Author.
>
> This program was directed by Jessica Kaye and produced by Top Producer.
>
> Text copyright 2020 by Master Author; Production Copyright 2020 by Best Audiobook Publisher, Incorporated.
>
> All Rights Reserved.

The intro will be the first thing heard on your audiobook recording, unless you use music to open your program. Similarly, the outro will be the last thing the listener hears, again unless you have music at the end of the program. The music may last a bit longer than either the intro or the outro. Not every producer chooses to use music. Many, maybe even most, do not. It is a personal choice. It can even depend on what the audiobook is about because some practically beg for music. Imagine recording a biography of Beethoven and not having a little Moonlight Sonata or his well-known Fifth Symphony, or any other of his compositions to enhance the subject of the book.

In case you were wondering, the reason I record both the intro and the outro first thing rather than recording the outro at the end is to ensure that we do not forget to record it. There have been occasions, thankfully few, in which the exhaustion and exhilaration of finishing recording have aided and abetted in forgetting to record the outro. Just do it first thing. That way, when you reach the end of your book, you really are done. If it turns out you mispronounced someone's name or otherwise erred in recording the credits, then do record them again somewhere during the recording session, whether at the end or otherwise.

How Do I Find Music for My Audiobook?

If you choose to use music or sound effects in your audiobook, whether at the start and close or sprinkled throughout, just as with licensing art for your cover or the rights to the book itself, you need to find the owner of the music you wish to use and obtain a license, in writing. You will need to perform the conditions of that license. That means paying the agreed fee, obviously, but there may be other limitations, such as territorial ones or giving a credit on the recording or the packaging. If you are planning to distribute your audiobook worldwide, be sure that your music license gives you the right to worldwide use.

There are numerous *music libraries* that license music cues for a fee or even for free. A few of them are listed in the Resources section of this book. You can use a search engine to find more options or ask others in the industry for their recommendations. A *music library* is the term given to define companies with collections of pieces of music that can be licensed to people and companies who need music for their productions, whether audio or audio/visual.

In-Studio Best Practices

In the studio, I wear headphones and I suggest you ask your director to do so, too. This is so that you not only hear your narrator clearly, but you also hear other sounds that do not belong on your recording. You want to be able to steer clear of the extraneous noises you now know about, such as stomach noise, excessive mouth noise, sirens, your narrator's foot accidentally kicking the music stand on which the script lies, dogs barking, helicopters or airplanes overhead, a bracelet jangling, lawn mowers. Your goal is to have as pristine a recording as possible. Listening via headphones will help to achieve that goal.

There is not uniform agreement about whether the narrator should also wear headphones. Some directors prefer to have narrators work without them. The cord can hit the microphone stand and add noise that can be avoided without headphones. Another reason is some directors and producers believe the distraction of hearing one's own voice is not worth having them wearing the headphones. I lean toward the latter camp but either way is fine. Just be sure to keep alert for those extra noises that can come from creaky ear pads or the cord.

When you do hear a noise, hit the talk-back button and tell your narrator you need to do that line, or part of the line, again. If you choose to do just part of the line, make sure you recommence recording somewhere in the script where there was a natural pause, so that your editor can make a clean edit. Mark the script wherever you hear a noise so that the editor can clean it up, if possible. You can use the letter N to indicate there is *noise*. That saves you from writing the word noise; although it is a short word, by the time you have finished writing it, the narrator has moved on and you may have missed something else that happened, such as a retake, a stumble, or yet another noise.

There are at least two ways to record for retakes. One way is colloquially referred to as *punch and roll*. Using this method, the recording is taken back to a few seconds prior to the place where the disruption occurred. Upon rolling again, the narrator and director will hear a few moments of *playback* of the recording preceding where the voice talent needs to come in again. Playback means exactly what it sounds like. You play back some of what you have recorded. Here's an example. The sentence is "John got up and walked to the kitchen." Just as the narrator said the word *walked*, a loud noise came from outside. Let's say someone slammed a door and it reverberated into the studio. The engineer will roll the recording back to the last few words prior to "John got up ..." and so the narrator will hear the end of the preceding phrase and will know that when it ends, it is time for her to begin narrating again. This way, the recording is semi-edited as you go because the new take is the keeper and the earlier takes are eliminated. The result of this style of retakes is that when the recording gets to the editor, she will have fewer takes to edit.

The way I prefer to work is to have the computer continue to roll even when we have to do a retake and have the editor take out the extraneous noises later. I do this because although the editing process will require more work and more time, the narrator is able to continue without waiting for us to roll back, listen back, and then come in again. Though others may have differing opinions, my feeling is that the voice talent is less encumbered and can jump right back into the narration with continuous roll. You will simply use your talk-back button to let him know you need to do a retake. Often, I will explain the reason why and other times the narrator will ask. Occasionally, after we have established a working relationship, I may ask for a retake without giving the reason. Sometimes it is because I have sensed that the narrator is already aware of the reason and sometimes it is just to be expeditious. Sometimes it is because I have simply forgotten to share the reason. Often the narrator will realize there has been an error and will do the retake before I even reach for the talk-back button.

A talk-back button, by the way, can take various forms but it is what allows you to speak with your narrator. It means an interruption to your reader, but it is necessary. You want to rerecord anywhere those noises occurred. This is always important, but even more so if your narrator will not be available to return to record pickups after the audiobook has been edited and QC'd.

When you get to the studio and are settled in to where you will be seated during the session, make sure to ask the engineer where your talk-back button is. If you don't know how it works, ask her to explain. You can't know what something is or how to use it until you have tried it for yourself. If you are directing remotely, via Skype or some other method, your talk-back button is usually just your mute button on your phone, tablet, or computer, which you will mute and unmute as needed. You want to be muted except when you are speaking with the narrator and engineer so that no noise from your location will get into the recording. A pristine recording is the goal. If you aren't hooked up electronically into the narrator's booth or headphones, you will relay your concerns to the in-studio engineer. This is a bit like playing the old-fashioned game of telephone, where you tell someone something and the someone you told tells it to the next person. It is not particularly efficient, but occasionally it is all you have to work with.

At times, the talk-back button may not be working. Test it with your narrator before you begin to record. If it isn't working, the engineer will do whatever is necessary to get it to work. It happens. If it isn't working, that is an impediment to the recording process because your narrator, at best, will be separated from you by glass and walls, and will be looking at the script—not at you—so hand signals won't be seen. Many studios have setups where you and the narrator can't even see each other, which rules out all visuals, so if the talk-back isn't working, either you need to be very creative or postpone the session until the talk-back is fixed. As with many other glitches, this is rare but be aware that it can happen.

There are other reasons to use the talk-back button. There may be issues in the book that you want to discuss with the talent and/or with the engineer. Recording an audiobook is a collaborative process. If there are questions about inflection or whether something jibes or doesn't jibe with earlier content, it's worth discussing, unless you have already determined how you want to handle it in your preparation for the session. If you have not yet told your reader what you want her to do at any particular point, when you reach that point, break in to let her know. This can be how to pronounce a word, which character's voice to use, what the inflection should be, whether to use an American or other accent at any particular point, or other issues which may arise.

Here is how your session will go, from start to finish: The software will roll, the narrator will be given the signal to begin and will read until stopped for any reason, whether by himself or at your intervention due to an error. It's pretty straightforward. With a seasoned engineer at the helm, any issues with equipment should be fixable. As we discussed, some combination of you and the narrator and the author and the publisher can fix text-based issues.

When I direct, I mark the time code on the top of nearly every page. The time code is where you are in the session. If you are recording in Pro Tools, ask the engineer to put the Big Counter up on the screen. Yes, it is actually called the "Big Counter," and it will make it easier for you to keep an eye on the time code.

Why do you want to track the time so closely? There are a few reasons. First, you may need to reference the location of something in the recording. Suppose you have a word that comes up more than once, and you are unsure how you said it the first time. You can go back to listen to that segment of the recording easily if you mark the session and the time code on each (or most) pages. You search the manuscript, which is particularly easy if you are using an electronic manuscript and if not, then a manual search will have to do. Oh, there it is on page 12, which began at 35:12 (thirty-five minutes and twelve seconds into the recording session). You know this because you wrote 35:12 at the top of the page. By eyeballing the time at the top of page 12 and noting how far down the page your word occurs, you can estimate the approximate time where you will find the audio segment, then play it back and know how you said it and whether it was correct or you need to do a pickup. By the way, I have been referring to pickups as recording done after the audiobook sessions, but can also take place before the audiobook recording is completed.

If your editor is "chasing the recording," or editing files from one session while you are working on another, so that they are not far behind you in their work, the editor may send you a list of pickups to record while you still have the narrator handy, during the initial recording sessions of the book. The things an attentive editor will notice include misreads, slurred words, noises she cannot edit out, and maybe even sections that were inadvertently unrecorded. This happens more often than you may think. Sometimes during a session we stop to have a discussion and afterward continue recording in the wrong place, not realizing we have skipped a sentence or a paragraph simply by restarting too far down the page. Thank goodness for the editors who notice and let you know. You can ask your editor to do this if she is chasing the recording.

Sometimes a director will zone out or be busy making a note for the editor or even for herself, and be unsure whether there were any errors in the recording that occurred during the time she was making that note. The time code will come in handy here, too, so that either on a break or even during the session, if the director breaks in to the recording to explain she needs to listen back, she can play the section that was recorded while she was otherwise engaged, to make sure it is free of errors. She can also mark retakes and noise and anything else pertinent to the editor that was missed initially.

Another use for marking the time code at the top of each page is for when you and the narrator have had a conversation off the record and the equipment has been paused. If you have forgotten to roll recording again once your chat is through, when you look up for the time code to put at the top of the next page, you will see you are not rolling. While it is frustrating to the talent and to the director to have gone forward with the narration without engaging the recording, the good news is that you will not have gone too far into the text. Your narrator will have to reread whatever he started with postconversation, but it should be no more than a page, if you are religiously using the time code system.

I mentioned errors with recording software. It is not unusual to find that the recording stopped without anyone noticing. Often this is a simple fix and the engineer can have you up and going in a short time. This is another good reason to mark the time code on the top of each page, because if the software stops and you are marking the time at the top of nearly every page, you will see when you next look up to mark the time code that in fact the software has suffered a glitch and you are no longer rolling. Otherwise, it could be pages and pages before anyone notices that you have not been recording. That is not only likely to make for a very unhappy narrator but also is a waste of studio time—for which you are paying.

Room Tone

At least once during your recording sessions, ask the engineer to record room tone. Room tone is simply the ambient sound of the recording booth. Typically room tone is recorded for about a minute or less. The narrator is not in the room during this time. The reason to record room tone is so that the editor can match the room's sound when editing, to keep the sound consistent. It is also used at the start and finish of each audiobook file to lead in and exit from the narration. Remember to record it during your first session so that your editor has it on hand when she starts editing. Mark the room tone's placement on both the script and on the audio file so that the editor can easily find it.

Room tone is usually recorded just once during an audiobook recording but it can be recorded more often if needed. It is needed if you have more than one narrator, in which case you should get room tone for each narrator as the ambient sound may be different for each. Record room tone for each booth you use if you record in more than one room or have changed any settings in the equipment in the recording booth.

The Editor

The audio files, your director's script, and sometimes the engineer's marked script, too, will be sent to the editor, typically on a daily (or more than once daily) basis. Some publishers like to have the audio files and director's script sent to the editor twice daily: once at the lunch break and once at day's end.

You find an editor in much the same way you found your studio, your director, and your narrator: Use the resources available to you, such as networking, asking others who they have used and like and recommend, seeing if there are editors listed on the APA (Audio Publishers Association) website, using a search engine on the internet. Any of these or a combination of them should result in at least a shortlist of editors you can approach about your project. Ask if they are available and interested in your gig. Ask what they charge. If you don't already have a recommendation or two for their work, you can ask for references.

The editor counts on having a marked script so that she can see where retakes are, where there are noises to cut out, and other important information, like which take you want her to keep if it isn't the last take. Maybe the narrator has a lot of mouth noise and you want to warn the editor of that as an overall note. If you are using a tablet to mark the script, sometimes the software will experience a glitch, and you may want to note that to the editor once it is up and running again—in case you were unable to mark the script during a portion of the session. This happens fairly frequently. It is one of the few drawbacks to using an iPad or similar electronic device. The advantages over paper include the ability to instantly transmit the marked script to the engineer by email or uploading to an FTP or other server; to save paper and ink; and also, the reduction of noise that would otherwise come from turning pages.

If you have used a paper script, then you will need to scan and email it to the editor, or deliver it to her somehow, whether handing it over physically or popping it into FedEx or the mail. How quickly you send your paper script might depend on what your overall schedule is for editing, QC'ing and recording pickups, if any, and, ultimately, releasing the audiobook. If you do send it by mail or courier, make a copy of it so that if it gets waylaid, you still have a copy of your marked script. This is easy to do by scanning it and uploading or emailing it to yourself.

Song Lyrics

Many books quote song lyrics or refer to a melody. A good practice is to have the narrator read the lyrics rather than sing them. The reason for this is that typically a writer or his publisher will have cleared the right to include lyrics in the book, but that clearance almost certainly does not include the right to perform the song. Performance rights are separate from the right to reprint lyrics. Play it safe and don't let your narrator sing.

I already hear you saying, "Yes, but what if …" There are a few "what ifs" that might carve out exceptions to this rule. There are "what ifs" that carve out exceptions to nearly every rule. Unless you know that the song is from the nineteenth century and is not protected by copyright, or you have written permission from the performance rightsholder to sing on the recording, do not do it. This rule is for your own safety.

Pickups

If you have not asked the narrator whether she will be able to return to the studio in the event that pickups are necessary, ask her at the session. Pickups should be considered part and parcel of the gig. On occasion, I have been asked whether the narrator will be additionally compensated for doing pickups. The answer is that usually she will not. This is true whether she is being paid a flat rate for the gig or a per finished hour (PFH) rate. Pickups are standard and included in the narrator's work. The exception to this might be if there is an unusually high number of pickups that were not the fault of the narrator. This could be due to an inattentive director, a technology glitch, or a script that turns out to be vastly different from the final version of the book—and the audiobook was recorded prior to receipt of that final manuscript.

As far as a technology glitch goes, it is always a good idea to have a backup recording running to protect against just this sort of problem. Not every studio is able to provide backup, but try to have that available whenever possible. This way, if the hard drive fails or experiences some other problem, you can provide the backup recording to the editor and save yourself from having to pay the studio and the narrator for additional hours if the glitch means they will have to spend a fair amount of time back in the recording booth.

The Workday

How many hours will the narrator work at one time? As with so many things, the answer varies. Often a studio day will run from 10 A.M. to 4 P.M., but that depends on the availability and stamina of the narrator, the availability of the studio, the length of the book, and whether anyone has an appointment that cuts into the day. Some narrators prefer to start earlier and/or stay later. I worked with one narrator who liked to start at 7:00 A.M. because she lived far away from the studio and this allowed her to avoid rush hour. That was fine with me; I like mornings, but it will not be fine for every director. It is quite typical for the work to go six to eight hours per day, with breaks for lunch and to get some air and to walk around a bit, make phone calls, and check email. How long your sessions go and for how many days is also a function of the urgency of the project. Is the audiobook supposed to publish simultaneously with the hard copy about to hit the stores? If so, the recording sessions need to be timely in order to get the recorded sessions to the editor, then to QC, and then back to the studio if pickups are needed and back again to the editor if a second round of edits is needed.

How many days to schedule also depends on how many hours per day you are working and the skill of the team, especially the narrator, but I have occasionally felt hampered by an inexperienced engineer or one who does things differently than I do. My general goal is to have enough recorded to result in three finished, i.e., edited, hours' worth of material per day. If we work an extra-long day, I want to end up with more than three hours of finished material. The finished time of a day's work isn't something you can know for certain while you are recording; you just use your past experience to estimate what you will have at the end of the day. Directors new to the studio may not be able to guesstimate the day's result, but in time they will learn to have a feel for it.

MULTIVOICE READERS

If you have more than one narrator, plan to record them separately. The exception is if you absolutely need the interplay of them speaking at the same time, as when they speak over each other. Book separate recording sessions for each. This is in order to minimize noise during each session to produce a clean recording, as we've discussed. This is not a hard-and-fast rule, but it is a useful guideline.

An example of numerous narrators recorded separately is *Lincoln in the Bardo* by George Saunders. The producer, Kelly Gildea of Penguin Random House, worked with 166 narrators to ensure each character in the book was given a distinctive voice. It was a creative choice and the audiobook has been lauded, winning the 2018 Audie Award for Audiobook of the Year.

You will need your editor's help to figure out how to pay narrators on a multivoice project because you will need to calculate how many minutes each narrator performed if they are being paid on a PFH basis. This is where your elementary school mathematics will come in handy. You know each narrator's hourly rate. Take the hourly rate and divide it by sixty to determine the rate per finished minute. Then multiply that rate per minute by the total number of minutes for each reader's time on the recording, which your editor has supplied to you. That is how much that reader has earned. Do the same for each of the voices on your project. When you have finished, check your math by multiplying the total time by the rate. It should balance. If it doesn't, try it again.

STUDIO FOOD AND DRINK

If you are spending a number of hours at a time at the studio, you should either provide meals and snacks or advise your talent to bring food to the session. At a minimum, provide tea, coffee, and water. If you are working in a studio you do not own, check ahead of time to find out what amenities they have. If you do provide lunch, it is a nice gesture to include the engineer. That's just common courtesy. Yes, it is an additional expense, but it isn't much of one.

Another issue about meals is whether to go out or to order in. My preference is to order in because you can continue working until your food arrives and you save the time of going somewhere, waiting to order, waiting for your meal, and returning to the studio. Sometime in the mid- to late-morning ask what type of food your voice talent would like to order and see if the studio can provide local menus. In many cities, you don't even need to have someone run out to pick up the order or choose a restaurant merely because it delivers. With apps such as Postmates or Uber Eats, you have a wider range of restaurants from which to choose.

Sometimes a performer will express a strong desire to go out at lunchtime. Let him. The director may go with him if he is amenable to her company, or he may just want an hour alone, without the director or engineer. That is okay. Do set a firm time to resume recording and even with that firm time agreed to, expect to start up late. If everyone is back on time, that's terrific, but it doesn't always happen. Save yourself a little bit of aggravation by being prepared for that eventuality.

There will be other breaks besides meal breaks. Every sixty to eighty minutes or so, even if things are going swimmingly and neither of you wants to take a break, suggest one. There is research to suggest that standing every hour or so, stretching, maybe walking around outside a bit (if it is safe to do so), and using the restroom—anything to stand and step away from the microphone and out of the booth—is good for both the brain and the body. It is good for the director, too. It may feel as though the team is burning time, but they may burn more time later if you do not allow for breaks. The diminishing returns will speak for themselves.

HOME RECORDING

An important and large trend over the past decade or so is that many narrators often record at home, without the presence of an engineer or a director. This may be something you will want to utilize. Generally, you will still pay the narrator a fee based on finished hours, but you will save the expense of both the studio and the director. Note I did not say you are saving the expense of the engineer because most of the time, the engineer's fee is built into what the studio is charging. With a home studio, the narrator acts as her own engineer and has configured the recording booth so that she has a means by which she can control the computer, which is outside the booth. Why is it outside of the booth? In part because most computers emit noise and in part to minimize the clutter in the booth, where space is often at a premium.

You need to know what type of file you will receive from the narrator: Will she deliver files that are edited but unmastered, edited and mastered, or unedited? If they will deliver edited and mastered files, be sure to ask to listen to samples now and again. Ask to hear fifteen minutes from the first day before they move into day two. If there are issues with the recording, you can nip things in the bud by listening early. If you are unsure of what the sample should sound like, do yourself a favor: Hire someone with experience in producing or directing audiobooks to listen to the clip for you. It shouldn't cost much and can save you a great deal of time and money. If you end up with something you consider subpar, then you are in a pickle, especially if your publication date is imminent. An ounce of prevention is worth a pound of cure.

If you are going to use a self-directing, self-recording narrator, it serves you well to hire someone who has significant experience in the audiobook business. Otherwise, you are helping someone to reinvent the wheel and that someone, sadly, is not just the narrator but also you. Additionally, a recording made without a director needs to be QC'd to ensure inflection and tone are appropriate, and to mark intrusive noises, if any, and advise you of pickups that are needed.

WHAT NARRATORS WANT PUBLISHERS TO KNOW

Cassandra Campbell is a lauded narrator with hundreds of audiobooks to her credit. Her beautiful voice and command of language keep her work calendar full. I asked her if she had anything she wanted publishers to know about narrators who work from a home studio. She did.

When a narrator works for one of the major publishers, usually she has a director who is following along and can let her know if a pronunciation is off or if the inflection is not quite right. Someone is editing the audiobook as fast as the studio sends the sessions to them. This is to make publishing deadlines. If the editor picks up on any errors or glitches, he can let the director know and the narrator can rerecord those lines before the sessions are concluded. Then, once the audiobook has been edited and sent to QC, the notes of any pickups are sent to the narrator.

But when the narrator records from home, she is her own director and there is no second set of eyes and ears. She sends the audio files to the editor and usually does not hear back from him with pickups she can record right away, often not even before the title goes to QC. The problem for the narrator is that if any error is a big error, such as an incorrect accent or a word that appears multiple times and is mispronounced multiple times, there is a lot of extra time involved in rerecording.

Cassandra's advice to publishers is to ensure someone is listening to what the narrator has recorded as quickly as possible; preferably while she is still recording. This would provide a safety net for catching big errors early.

Home studios are a wonderful thing because they enable narrators to choose their own hours so long as the work is turned in on time, they can save publishers the cost of renting or building a recording studio, and they allow a publisher to record a number of books at one time due to the reasonable cost and the lack of the need to provide premises for performing the work.

MASTERING THE RECORDING

Now that your audiobook has been recorded, edited, been through quality control, and, if needed, had its second or third edit—however many you need—it will be mastered. If your editor is providing you with a mastered recording, then you are all set. If you need to find someone other than the editor to handle this part of readying your project for publication, it is possible your editor can make a referral. If not, you will use the same process for finding professionals as you used before: network, get recommendations, ask others in the business if they can provide names.

What Is Mastering?

Dan Musselman, a longtime producer and engineer in the recording arts, including his long and ongoing stint in audiobooks with Penguin Random House, explained *mastering* as bringing the recording into sync with industry specs and making it sound good.

In layperson's terms, the idea is to adjust the levels as needed so the high pitches don't sound too high, the low pitches don't sound too low, and the recording isn't too loud or too quiet. The goal is that the program will have dynamic range: There will still be louder and quieter sections, but they will be brought more to the middle, to keep them closer to the average level, which is easier on the ears. If the audiobook recording is of good quality, very little processing is needed for mastering.

Mastering also includes breaking the audiobook into sections, typically chapter by chapter, and naming the tracks. This is true both for CD and for digital delivery systems. Some books do not have chapters, in which case the sections are divided into segments by time. Some books have long chapters and for these, a long chapter with several segments will be named 1a, 1b, and so on, as needed.

The industry leader for digital delivery is Audible.com, so most publishers use Audible's specs (meaning their delivery requirements) to master their recordings. This eliminates having to master the recording differently for different markets, whether hard copy or other digital download providers.

Once the mastering is completed, you are ready to publish your audiobook!

How do you do *that*?

SUMMARY

This was an advanced beginner's class in audiobook production. You learned about prepping your narrator, whether to use headphones for both the director and the talent, getting materials to the editor, pickups, whether to use music. You heard from Cassandra Campbell about how publishers and home narrators can work together more efficiently, and you learned what mastering your audiobook means. Now on to the main event. Let's get your audiobook out into the world.

CHAPTER 9

Getting Your Audiobook to Market and Marketing Your Audiobook

Getting your audiobook to market is not the same thing as marketing your audiobook. But you need to do both of these things in order to be a successful publisher.

PACKAGING HARD COPY

If you are selling CDs or other hard copies, you need to manufacture and package them. What type of packaging do you want to use? Take a look at what other audiobook publishers do for packaging and see what appeals to you. If you find that a company uses packaging that you'd like to use, you can reach out to them to ask for a referral to their vendor. Most publishers would not be offended by that inquiry.

You can also use a search engine to find audiobook packaging and CD replication companies. Or go to the Audio Publishers Association website (www.audiopub.org) and do some research there. The Resources list at the back of this book can also help.

You do not need to have everything made at the same place. Packaging companies can send the printed packages to your CD replicator, which can manufacture your CDs and insert them into the packages and shrink-wrap them. Shop around for pricing and for the type of packaging you like, but also check out the companies' reputations. Ask for references, and ask around the industry. It's possible to stay with a manufacturer for years if you are happy with them; sometimes you will change the companies making your components. Sometimes you will have multiple vendors so that you are not wholly reliant on a single resource. The adage not to put your eggs in one basket is a good one. A manufacturer could have economic troubles or a work slowdown or broken equipment or a power failure. If you are publishing a number of audiobook titles, you'll want to find a good CD replicator and a good packaging company—once you do, you should look for a second one you can depend on as well. Options are fewer than when CDs were the predominant medium on the market, but you can still find enough companies to work with.

Generally, if you are selling into bookstores, you will need to get an International Standard Book Number, commonly known as ISBN, for each edition of your audiobook. That is, your CD needs an ISBN, and if you have vinyl or some other physical format as well, it will need its own ISBN too. If you reissue your audiobook in a new jacket or format, it will require a separate ISBN. The downloadable version may need an ISBN, depending on the companies with which you work. Most of them are able to take your downloadable audiobooks even without an ISBN number.

In the United States, you will get your ISBNs from a company called Bowker. The URL for ordering an ISBN is www.bowker.com/products/ISBN-US.html. You will pay for ISBNs, and the cost per ISBN goes down if you purchase multiples. If you are planning to purchase more than one audiobook, you probably should obtain more than one ISBN at a time (you do not need to know what titles will be assigned which numbers). It's good to have ISBNs on hand when you need them. For your physical products, you will use the ISBN in your bar code, which is also obtainable from Bowker.

CD BABY AND PRINT ON DEMAND FOR AUDIOBOOKS

Some publishers primarily distribute digitally but use CD Baby for Print-on-Demand CDs when they have a customer who wishes to own hard copy. That way there is no outlay for manufacturing except upon receipt of an order. It is similar to Print on Demand for books. CD Baby lists audiobooks in the genre "Spoken Word," so if you search the site for how to sell your audiobook, start with that. CD Baby can be found at www.cdbaby.com.

TIMING THE MARKET

The timing of your release can be important to the sales and visibility of your title. We have already talked a little about tie-ins with movie releases or other events. Audiobooks do not often have a budget that includes much money for advertising or promotion. I'll reiterate the notion that if you can capitalize on the publicity attendant on something else, whether the hardcover release of the book, a high profile social event, or anything else that's attracting the public's attention, it benefits you to have your release coincide with that.

What are your plans for selling your audiobook? I know, your plans are that you will sell umpteen million copies and retire to the Berkshires with a pied-à-terre in Manhattan. Those are not the plans I mean. Where and how are you planning to sell your audiobook? Those are the essential questions.

There are a variety of markets for audiobooks. There is the downloadable market, including notable venues such as Audible, iTunes, Kobo, and Audiobooks.com, among others. If you wish to sell directly to consumers, there is the hard copy market, which involves having a physical location, a phone number, or a website where customers can order CDs. If getting your CDs into stores is part of your plan, you need a way to do that. We covered back-of-the-room sales earlier and that may involve you bringing products to the event, or perhaps the event planner will order your CDs from a wholesaler. Many libraries carry audiobooks, both in hard copy and downloads. There are services that stream audiobooks. Choose your formats and then figuratively draw a map of how to get your product to your customers.

DISTRIBUTION

If you don't have a way to get your audiobook in front of prospective buyers, you can't have sales. You need to get distribution.

There are various ways to accomplish this. If you are already a book publisher, find out if your current distributor can also handle audiobooks. Decide whether you are going to manufacture hard copy or limit your sales to electronic distribution only. Your current distributor may be knowledgeable about the landscape for audiobook sales in either or both formats, and in that case, listen to what they have to say. If you do choose to sell CDs, or any form of hard copy, then a traditional distributor may be your best bet in terms of getting product onto store shelves. Some distributors may be able to handle both hard copy and electronic versions for you. Some may be limited to only one format.

If you do not already have a publishing company and you want to sell CDs or some other hard copy format, you need to find a company to present your line to retail outlets. An organization that can help you identify likely companies for distributing your work is the Independent Book Publishers Association (IBPA). This trade group has been in existence for a few decades and has a number of resources to help both new and seasoned independent publishers. Their website address is www.ibpa-online.org.

There are not a great many independent distributors nowadays. One company that does handle a large number of publishers is called Independent Publishers Group (IPG). There are also Ingram Content Group, Baker & Taylor, and Publishers Group West (PGW). There are some others. You know the drill by now. Network and ask around. Don't be afraid to contact trade organizations or take a look at their websites to see if they shed light on any of your questions or issues.

One more word of advice here: Choose carefully. Your contract is likely to be for a specific term so it behooves you to check references to determine whether a particular distributor's clients are happy with the service they are receiving.

BOOK TRADE DISCOUNT RATES

If you choose to be self-distributing, when you sell an audiobook, or any type of book, know that retailers are used to receiving a discount from the retail price. They have to get a discount, because if they paid full retail price, they would not make any money by selling that same item to a customer. There are exceptions on either side of the retail discount rates, but for the most part, publishing industry discounts fall between 30 to 60 percent. When you get to the high end of the discount rates, you are either selling to someone who has very superior bargaining power, a megastore, for example, or you are making what are known as *nonreturnable sales*. We touched on this in Chapter 2. *Nonreturnable sales* are just what they sound like. The customer is buying audiobooks from you that they are not allowed to return. This is unlike most of the book trade, with its returnable discount rates, and it is a rare bright spot of a sale staying a sale. You give the customer a large discount, and in exchange they waive their right to return product. Most of the book and record venues that sell hard copies will not agree to a nonreturnable deal.

What if you want to be your own distributor? This is challenging. Many stores will not purchase from a single, small publisher because they don't know you and have no track record with you, and because they need to know that if they make returns to you, you will appropriately credit their account or refund their money. Once over that hurdle, if you are self-distributing, you will have to set your discount schedule. Stores will be invoiced at that discount schedule. Some stores will insist on larger discounts than other stores and depending on their bargaining power, may get them. You may wish to consult with an attorney to determine the law so that if you are providing different treatment to different *classes of customers*, you are not violating any laws in the process. Classes of customers are simply customers who are similar to other customers, such as single-store bookstores, small chain bookstores, large chain bookstores. The class of customer will determine where the customer fits in your discount schedule. For example, a store ordering a few *units* receives a lower discount than a store ordering hundreds or thousands of units. A *unit* means a single piece of product. Treat like customers alike so that you do not find yourself accused of discriminatory practices.

If you do have a distributor, they already will have their discount rates in place and you will want to know what they are so that you can analyze your sales reports to ensure accuracy and your comprehension of them. Don't worry, it isn't a secret they will keep from you. Your distributor will advise you on what the discount rates are to the different classes of customer. You will also see it on the sales reports they send you.

ELECTRONIC DISTRIBUTION

If you wish to distribute electronically only, or need a secondary distributor to handle this format, you also have some options. I would be remiss in not mentioning my own digital distribution company for audiobooks, Big Happy Family, LLC (www.big happyfamilyaudio.com). Other options include trying to go direct with download sites or using another distributor. Once again, the Audio Publishers Association (www.audiopub.org) may come in handy. Its membership list includes distribution companies, so take a look and make inquiries about each one to determine which is the best fit for your line.

Even if you do have a distributor, you should educate yourself about the various venues for downloads or other electronic transmissions. As a business owner, you need to know who your customers are. It matters where your materials end up, if for no other reason than for you to be able to tell prospective customers where they can find your audiobooks. Libraries, for instance, are a popular place for consumers to obtain audiobooks, so you will want to know which companies distribute to libraries.

AUDIOBOOK DELIVERY FORMATS

Think of all the ways people obtain audiobooks and do a little research to help yourself become informed about the sales landscape for your new products. Your company's audiobooks may determine the best methods of delivery. For example, Michele Cobb, currently the executive director of the APA and also an audiobook publisher in her own right, has seen that in the global market, children's audio does better in places that still use CDs because a child cannot shop at most audiobook download sites, but a parent can either download an app for their child's use or buy CDs.

Along with knowing your formats and likely sales venues, it is useful to know how and where end users, your ultimate customers, are listening to audiobooks. Many people listen in their cars, while exercising, cooking, doing crafts, or any of a number of activities that allow them to multitask. A fair number listen at night at bedtime. Your customers are listening with earbuds or without, from their CD players, from their tablets. Many new cars do not include CD players and that will influence the sales figures of CDs. In many homes and offices, the smart speaker has become part of the furniture and is used for listening to audiobooks. It's always interesting to see what new delivery systems are coming down the pike, and how and where audiobook listeners are using our recordings.

WHAT YOUR DISTRIBUTOR WILL NEED FROM YOU

Distributors of hard copy audiobooks will need your products in their warehouses, of course. Once in a great while they may ask you to drop-ship an order. That means you will ship the order directly from your on-hand inventory or even from your manufacturer rather than sending the products to the distributor's warehouse. But this happens only in the rare case where you are doing a promotion with a customer or are close to or missing a publication date and the customer is eagerly awaiting the arrival of your hot commodity. Most of the time, the distributor will handle fulfilling orders.

A distributor will catalog your titles. If they are selling to stores, this is likely an actual catalog, whether printed or digital, so that store buyers have a chance to review the distributor's entire list of represented titles. In the case of a digital distributor, the catalog is more of a list or a digital booklet.

You will need to provide the distributor with metadata for each title. *Metadata* is defined as a set of data that describes and gives information about other data. In the publishing world, it is a list of the pertinent facts regarding your publications. The form on which this information is provided is, logically enough, called the metadata form. There is not one universal form; each distributor or download sales venue may have its own form, but the information requested tends to be similar. It usually includes the name of the audiobook, the author, the narrator, a description of the content, the running time, the copyright information and genre, usually listed in accordance with Book Industry Standards and Communications (BISAC) categories. BISAC provides a long list of categories into which book subject matters may fall; it is from that list you will probably identify your audiobook's subject. You can use more than one BISAC category to describe your audiobook. Your distributor will also need you to provide a JPEG of the cover art for display next to a description of the title on download sites.

Once you have provided information to your distributor they, in turn, will provide it to their customers, which are bookstores and other sales venues.

JESSICA'S FIFTH RULE OF AUDIOBOOK PUBLISHING

Promoting Your Audiobook

Congratulations on getting a distributor! Now that you have a way to get your audiobook into the hands and ears of customers, how can you let the world know that the title is out there awaiting them? That is something you, as the publisher, need to carefully determine. It is the publisher's job to promote its titles. It is the distributor's job to make those titles available for sale. Do you see the difference?

This is an important point. Some publishers seem to believe that by the simple act of making an audiobook available for purchase, there will be numerous purchases. Yet, your audiobook is one of many thousands published every year. How is a listener going to know about your product if you don't make some noise in the marketplace? This is my Fifth Rule of Audiobook Publishing: *It is the publisher's responsibility to market the audiobook.* There are myriad ways to do this and the rest of this chapter will help you consider some of them.

Advertising

Should you take out advertising to promote your audiobooks? Well, as with many things we have discussed, that depends. It depends on whether you have an available budget for advertising. It depends on whether you think you will get an adequate return on investment in advertising. It depends on whether there is an efficient and effective way to reach your target audience. It depends on what venue you are contemplating using. If, after thinking over these criteria, you believe advertising will be worthwhile, then by all means, advertise.

Where might you advertise the release of a new audiobook? There are magazines that review or write about audiobooks. This includes the publishing industry magazine *Publishers Weekly* which writes about audiobooks but does not review them and a related magazine titled *Library Journal*. Retailers and librarians, among others, read these, and so if you do intend to advertise, your target market likely subscribes to these, and your ad may or may not be cost effective in having a positive impact on sales. There is also *AudioFile*, the magazine entirely about audiobooks. I am not recommending advertising nor advocating against it, but simply letting you know the potential to advertise is out there.

For *all* expenses in this business, do a cost-benefit analysis. You cannot know whether advertising will recoup its costs in subsequent sales. It often does not. Consider that when you add advertising costs to your budget.

Promoting Outside of Advertising

Aside from advertising, how else might you promote your new release? There are numerous ways to get the word out through electronic media. Some of these potential venues include bloggers and reviewers, as well as whatever the current favorite social media sites are at the time you are prepping the release of your audiobook. At the moment, those sites include Facebook, Instagram, Twitter, Pinterest, and Snapchat. You should be building your online presence so that when you are reaching out for media coverage or making an announcement, you have some impact on a prospective audience.

It's a good idea to create a blog, either for your company as a whole or for the authors you publish. The authors can take turns writing for the company blog, if they are willing to do so. You can invite guest bloggers from all facets of your publishing program to write, too. Have them write about something that ties in to what you are doing or to things of particular interest to you and your readership. Keep the blog fresh with new posts on a regular basis. Consider contributing a guest blog post on someone else's blog.

See if you can be a guest on someone's podcast or radio program. Most likely there is at least one program with a theme that is somehow related to your new release.

Consider uploading samples of your audiobooks to SoundCloud. SoundCloud has become a viable resource for allowing listeners to preview the work. SoundCloud does not sell the recordings, but it does permit the publisher to add a Buy link, which will take the customer to a site that does sell it. Take a little time to see the various listings publishers have uploaded there. Consider how that might come in handy for you, to aid visibility and be a place to host samples of your recordings for anyone to listen to.

There are a number of online communities that talk about audiobooks or are comprised of audiobook industry professionals. Seek them out. Some may require you to request admission to the group. That's okay; lots of groups do that just to make sure the people in it are all participants in the focus of the community. A good example of using Facebook in this way includes groups called "Audiobook Community" and "Audiobook Crowd."

This guidebook isn't about this subject, and I'm no expert on it, but it is important that you become comfortable with having an online presence. By presence, I don't mean you have to have your name or face out there. Unless you are the main commodity of your business, such as both publisher and author, you don't need to be visible, but your company and your audiobooks do. There are prospective customers who would love to listen to your audiobook but won't because they haven't heard of it or your company. That is fixed by making sure that word gets out about it. Of course, even publicity doesn't necessarily translate into sales, but raising your profile is the only way anyone will get to know of your publishing ventures short of sheer luck or stumbling over them while shopping for something to listen to.

I won't go into detail on how to build your platform, but in general, see what sites are of interest to you, which accounts tweet or post things you find pertinent—whether for fun or business—and start engaging. What makes social media social isn't just that it is out in public for anyone to see but that it can present forums for an exchange of ideas and information. You probably already know this but the basic rules of social media suggests that you don't use platforms to simply talk about yourself and your products every time you use it. That is not engaging; that is selling. First, build your audience. How? Read on.

Engaging doesn't mean that you never talk about what is in the pipeline for your company or what is in stores. It means that you talk about other things too. But be genuine. Surely you have more interests than just your audiobook. Consider what you talk about when you're face-to-face with people. Be engaging if you want your audience to be engaged with you.

Many resources can teach you how to be effective at promoting your company and books. Peruse your library's online catalog if you don't want to buy books. Don't feel guilty. Libraries are good customers of publishers. You may even find some books or other resources you want to purchase. I suggest, however, that you read reviews of a book before deciding whether or not to trust the advice in it.

Building a Platform

Jorjeana Marie is a successful actor, playwright, standup comic, teacher, and author of the nonfiction book *Improv for Writers: 10 Secrets to Help Novelists and Screenwriters Bypass Writer's Block and Generate Infinite Ideas* (Ten Speed Press, 2019). Jorjeana offers advice on what she calls building a platform, or building a presence so that your voice will be heard and your projects will be visible. Her advice is as applicable to audiobook publishers as it is to authors or businesspeople, or almost anyone in almost any profession. Jorjeana gave me this advice to pass along to you.

> There are different reasons for building a platform, initially, though I think most of them do end up at the sales doorstep eventually. I worked on my website for a long time as my main

showpiece to lead to work. Then I worked on building a platform to network and be able to present myself as a working, recommended professional, which I think is pretty important when someone on the other side of the world, or minimally, someone you've never met, is trying to decide to hire you, go with your service, etc.

When they can see that you have had a level of success, that your product is good, they feel safer betting on you.

Someone is always answering to someone else, and it's easier when they believe you are the solution. And they can believe it, when they see for themselves that your voice or your work has been the solution for someone else they have at least heard of. I got a lot of traction early on building my own business that way, leveraging the satisfaction of a job done as well as I could at the time with the tools I had at the time. And then I built from there, jockeying training with work, always learning, always upgrading the platform.

In publishing, the best social media one can invest their time in is one that is at the intersection of interest and demographics, like using Twitter because so many leaders in the publishing world are there, as well as target audience. *And*, you genuinely like hanging out on Twitter. I think you have to be a little inspired to be there. And also, I think it helps to make the content about other people at least part of the time, interacting and sharing and posting their material. I like when I get shares of things I've shared that mean something to me. They may not be about my project, but they are about something I care about and that I can connect with others on an issue that is still somehow related to me. It's a much better feeling than always: *Look at* MEEEEEE*!*

I think having a simple business plan, any plan, and starting to do the actions is incredibly helpful. But this is what's helpful for me. Writing things down is very important to me. Goals, lists, actions, gratitude. Pen to paper. But what works for you, what yields goodness for you, is the most important thing to understand and start implementing. And until then, experiment with websites, social media, content, coaches, etc. until you see a pattern and it becomes very clear. Because it will. And then you will be in the flow.

Jorjeana is right. You have to experiment with how to promote yourself, your company, your audiobooks, your publishing program. Once you learn the ropes and have had some success with promoting via social media, you will be able to adapt your platform as needed for each new audiobook you publish.

More Ways to Raise Your Profile

Karen Commins is a narrator, producer, publisher, consultant, blogger, and leading curator of information about the audiobook industry. She is very active in the audiobook community, especially online, and she has accumulated information about promoting the work, which she generously shares.

During an interview for this book, she noted that many authors fall into the dual traps of a) thinking the narrator will help promote the audiobook, and b) doing little to no promotion of it themselves.

A narrator has a different promotional mind-set and does not share the same goals as an author. Narrators generally publicize new releases, reviews, and awards in order to advertise their work and attract the interest of other people who might hire them. The author and/or publisher have the responsibility to increase sales.

Narrators usually are paid outright for their performances. If the narrator isn't earning royalties, he may have little incentive to promote a title past its release day. Even in cases where the narrator agreed to a royalty share contract with the author or publisher, his promotional efforts will still pale compared to those of the author and publisher—and that is as it should be. The publisher is selling the audiobook. It is true in commerce in general that the company selling a product is responsible for making the public aware of it.

Karen understands that new publishers and authors are inundated with a blizzard of advice, information, and courses about the latest and greatest social media site. A new platform seems to pop up every week, with a self-appointed expert teaching a class on it soon thereafter. Her advice is that audiobook publishers are best served by social media when they concentrate on just one or two sites and learn how to best use them to connect with their audience. The following questions will help to narrow your choices:

- Which site(s) do you enjoy using the most?
- Have you done any research to learn which sites your fans use and prefer?
- Are you planning to run ads?
- How much time will you make available to social media?
- Are you planning to schedule your posts?

By asking yourself these questions, you will naturally gravitate toward one or more platforms where you might experience the most success.

Beyond social media, Karen suggests the following eleven easy things you can do to update your followers about your audiobooks.

1. If you are the author or publisher of the underlying book, promote the book itself, as well as the audiobook. Also, include a link or a QR code for the audio edition on *every* piece of communication—newsletters, website, social media, postcards, bookmarks. The audiobook is only one edition of the book. No matter how someone searches for your book, they should see that an audiobook is available.

2. Try to ensure the audio edition appears on the same Amazon page as the other editions. If the audiobook is shown on an orphaned page, you can send an email to your contact at

Amazon to request that the editions be combined. Be sure to include the links to the Amazon pages for the audiobook and the Kindle and other editions.

3. Share different audio clips from the audiobook on your social media channels.

4. Write progress reports on your blog during audiobook production.

5. Add a blurb about or even a link to your audiobook in the front matter of your e-book, if you have one, and include the URL in your print books if you are the print publisher.

6. Encourage your author to have a website, if he doesn't already, and ask him to add a link to the audiobook sales site(s). Include the audiobook buy links from sales sites every time you mention the book on your website, blog, and social media or interviews, etc. Some authors even create landing pages specific to each audiobook that they then use in conjunction with Facebook and other paid ads.

7. Notify your email list about all new releases.

8. Create a promotional calendar for events throughout the year. Look through the yearly book *Chase's Calendar of Events* at your library or purchase a copy to have on hand. Also, search the Web to find evergreen tie-ins to your book's content that will give you reason to promote your title long past the release day. For instance, if your audiobook's heroine loves chocolate, you might give away the audiobook with some chocolate on October 28th, which is National Chocolate Day. By the way, June is audiobook month, so it's a great time to promote your audiobooks and build off of the industry's publicity efforts.

9. Conduct an audiobook event on Facebook to celebrate release day or some other occasion in your promotions calendar.

10. Host and record a video chat with your narrator and invite your fans and the narrator's fans to participate in the live stream. Fans love to have a look behind the scenes. Once the event is

over, post the video on YouTube. You and the narrator can then share the link to that video on your blogs and social media sites.

11. Audiobookboom.com is a weekly newsletter that highlights freebie audiobooks. Authors and publishers pay a small fee—ten dollars at the time of this writing—for a Listen & Review ad. That ad will be seen by audiobook listeners, who may request and review your audiobook in exchange for the free listening experience. The founder of the site, Jeffrey Kafer, is an experienced audiobook narrator who saw similar services working for e-books, giving rise to the idea for promoting audiobooks.

In case you are wondering why it makes sense to *give away* your audiobook when your intention is to *sell* it, the point is to grow reviews. Most publishers have a list of reviewers to whom they send their new publications. When a book is reviewed, more people become aware of it, and that can lead to increased sales. It is the same with audiobooks.

To grow your own list of reviewers, again see whether the APA website has any reviewers who are members. Send a review copy to *Audiofile* and other publications that review audiobooks. Cultivate bloggers, again by checking APA membership and doing an internet search for audiobook bloggers. Don't reach out to them without first familiarizing yourself with their blogs. If any of them align with what you are doing, then do reach out to them. After all, bloggers need things to write about. Be respectful, as always. If their blogs have ground rules for sending them information, follow those rules. If you do what they ask, it is a point in your favor toward getting them to do what you ask, whether that is to feature your company in an interview or publish a review or a promotion, or to pass along a press release to their followers. A good list of reviewers is cultivated over the years, and as you meet other publishers, some will share resources with you and you may share some with them. Keep the list fresh; cull the defunct ones from time to time.

Karen has many more good ideas about marketing and I recommend that you spend time on her website, which you'll find at www.karencommins.com. Her "Audiobook Marketing Cheat Sheet" can be found at www.AudiobookMarketingTips.com. You can learn a lot from people who have already tried or researched the very things you are wondering about. Karen's site features her own ideas, but she also links to a bounty of other sites that are relevant to you and your business.

Audio Clips on the Internet

Earlier, I briefly mentioned SoundCloud, a website allowing recording artists of all stripes to upload their work. You can upload samples of your programs, where people can listen to a bit of what you do. The company has added the ability to put a Buy Now button on your title's pages, so if someone hears something they like, they can buy it right away. That Buy Now button doesn't result in a purchase from SoundCloud. It will be linked to the purchase site of your choice, and the prospective buyer will be taken to that sales venue.

Carlyn Craig owns and is the publisher of Post Hypnotic Press, a Canadian audiobook company. She says they were the first audiobook publisher to start using SoundCloud and that they adopted it very early on. Their first and foremost reason for using it was as a way to provide audio clips on their own site; she is a fan of SoundCloud's "share," "embed," and "message" features.

She believes it has been very useful to promoting Post-Hypnotic Press's recordings. Carlyn said, "It's not that it, in and of itself, is a platform where people buy our audiobooks—although it can be—but that it provides a useful tool for sharing audio clips on social media. For instance, one can share to Twitter, Tumblr, and

Pinterest, and it creates a player so people can listen to the sample without leaving those sites."

She also likes the Buy button, although she is not sure that it has directly generated a lot of sales for her company. She thinks that may be due to the type of content they publish, which includes political, self-help, and other genres. "I think the promotional features of SoundCloud could be far more impactful for the popular genres in audiobooks," she said.

Carlyn also appreciates the statistics SoundCloud provides. They make information available in real time regarding the number of times a title was played, the number of likes it received, the number of reposts, and the number of comments and downloads. Carlyn says you can see where the listeners come from, by country. While the bulk of SoundCloud-hosted samples from Post-Hypnotic Press are played in the United States, she likes being able to see where else the audio clips have been played.

Publicists

Should you hire a publicist? In part, that is a personal decision, and in larger part, it is a business decision. Book publicists can help garner coverage for your audiobook, but will it be enough coverage to result in either a significant uptick in your company's visibility or sales of the audiobook? Will it be enough to make you happy you spent the money you did to hire her? I have never hired a publicist for anything my former publishing company published or for the company itself. That tells you the result of my cost-benefit analysis. I did not believe we would earn enough back to cover the costs of a publicist and so we never hired one. But that is only one person's evaluation.

You may come up with a different analysis. Maybe your pockets are deep or maybe your project is one exceptionally likely to catch the public's eye. As with anything else, do your due diligence.

Research publicists who have worked with audiobooks, see whether their clients have been pleased, find out whether any of their current clients are in the same industry you are in, and ascertain the cost of retaining the publicist and what they will do for that amount of money. Some will require that you sign on for a specific period of time, such as several months, with an agreed amount due each month. Find out what that amount is and do the math.

My last word on this subject is to honor those book publicists who work hard for their clients. I know some very good public relations (PR) people and I respect them. My opinion about the value of hiring someone to handle PR for one or a few audiobooks is not because these people aren't good at what they do. Many of them are very good at what they do. They are creatives with a virtual Rolodex, but I understand that they can only try to stir interest. They cannot force anyone to run a story about the recording or feature the author on a show. Results are not guaranteed, so if you do choose to hire a publicist, keep your expectations realistic. Know that everything you spend may be money out without commensurate money in.

AWARDS AND REVIEWS

Awards

Just as with film, television, print books, and radio, there are awards and reviews for audiobooks. Some of these are cost-free and some come with entry fees.

Do these awards and reviews have an impact on sales of the winners and nominees? It's hard to say, but it does seem likely there are at least incremental sales, however unmeasurable, for awarded titles, primarily because librarians are aware of most, if not all, of these awards, and libraries are an important sales venue for audiobooks. If a good review or an award can help get your audiobook into libraries, or into additional libraries, that is a good thing for your bottom line.

The most prestigious award as of this writing is the Grammy Award for Best Spoken Word recording. Grammy Awards are famous all over the world, and although Spoken Word is not a high-profile category, there are a number of high-profile winners that have garnered some good publicity for the category. Members of the organization called Recording Academy vote on the Grammys. Once you have credentials on a certain number of recordings, you can qualify for membership if you wish, and if you become a voting member, you are able to help determine which recordings bring home the statuettes. You can also submit your recordings for consideration. First, voting members are sent a preliminary ballot upon which every qualified submission is listed. From that initial vote, the field is whittled down to the finalists. Once the finalists are announced, the final ballot goes out. The votes get tallied and the Grammy is awarded.

Audie Awards are given annually by the Audio Publishers Association. Submissions are made by publishers and there is a per-submission fee. There are two rounds of judging. As with the Grammy Awards, the first round narrows down the entrants to the finalists. Unlike the Grammy Awards, members of the APA do not vote. The entries are judged by a panel carefully chosen by a committee of the board of directors of the Association.

The Earphones Award is a designation rather than something you can put on your shelf, although you can get a certificate to frame and hang on your wall. It is awarded by reviewers for *AudioFile Magazine*. According to *AudioFile* publisher, Michele Cobb, "The award is given by *AudioFile* to truly exceptional titles that excel in narrative voice and style, characterizations, suitability to audio, and enhancement of the text." She adds that the certificate is automatically sent to winners, if the magazine has the publisher's mailing address. If you noticed the similarity between the name of the publisher of *AudioFile Magazine* and the executive director of APA, you are right. Michele wears many hats in the audiobook world.

The Odyssey Award is given by the American Library Association (ALA) to the publisher of what the association judges the "best audiobook produced for children and/or young adults, available in English in the United States." There may be additional titles featured alongside the Odyssey winner. Those titles are called honor titles. The Odyssey Awards website, www.ala.org/alsc /awardsgrants/bookmedia/odysseyaward, has all the information you need about submitting audiobooks for consideration for the Odyssey and links to additional pages that describe their award process. One important thing to note: There is no charge for submitting audiobooks for consideration for the Odyssey Award.

A relatively new entry into the audiobook awards arena is the Voice Arts Awards, given out by the Society of Voice Arts and Sciences (SOVAS). This society was founded by voice-over artists to educate and award voice-over talent. There is a fee per entry per category. The awards are based on the decision of judges who listen to the submissions. Their judge-volunteering form requires the prospective judge to list their primary role in the voice-over industry, and it also requests the name and contact information of someone who can vouch for them. This should help ensure knowledgeable judging in the audiobook categories.

Reviews

Some magazines and newspapers regularly review audiobooks and/ or have audiobook best-seller lists, and there are some that cover the audiobook realm occasionally. A few you should know about, so that you can submit your audiobooks for review, are listed here.

- *AudioFile Magazine.* You already know that *AudioFile* designates some reviewed titles as Earphones Award winners. They review a great many audiobooks per issue, so even if your title doesn't win that designation, it will still be seen by many people, both consumers and librarians. That's a good thing unless, of course, your title receives a poor review.
- *Publishers Weekly* is a magazine for the publishing industry, containing contemporary information about trends, data, people, and companies in the publishing business. They do not review audiobooks at this time. They do report on the industry, however, so if there is something newsworthy about your audiobook or your company, send them a press release or reach out to their audiobook reporter.
- *Library Journal* reviews audiobooks and, as you may guess from its name, is helpful to librarians in finding titles on which to spend their budgets. Their guidelines for the submissions process are found at www.libraryjournal.com/?page=Review -Submissions. A good review may help you with library sales. Sometimes even a bad review is helpful, simply because it gets the name of your audiobook into public awareness. This is true even though it sounds unlikely.
- *School Library Journal* reviews audiobooks. Their home page is www.slj.com and, again as you probably guessed by the magazine's name, their primary reader is the school librarian. If your audiobook is school-age appropriate, try to have it reviewed in *SLJ*.

A long-time reviewer of audiobooks, Rochelle O'Gorman, has actively promoted the audiobook community because she loves the medium. She writes reviews for the *Los Angeles Times, Cleveland Plain Dealer,* and the *Christian Science Monitor,* as well as several smaller publications. She was the first syndicated audiobook reviewer in the United States, and she received an Audie Award for her contributions to the industry. Even if she doesn't review your audiobooks, it is worth reading what she writes by doing an online search because she does have a deep appreciation and knowledge of the industry. You are likely to learn something useful.

Crowdsourced Communities and Reviews

Amazon.com allows reviews of just about anything it sells. Amazon owns Audible.com. Audiobook reviews posted on Audible often make their way to the Amazon listing of the same audiobook. With any luck, your audiobooks will receive many good reviews and the huge worldwide audience that Amazon and Audible share might see those reviews. There are many audiobooks without reviews. It doesn't necessarily mean that no one is listening, as many people listen to audiobooks or read books without posting reviews. As I've said, good reviews can help sales, so encourage your customers to post reviews.

You have probably heard of Goodreads. It is a large online community of book readers and audiobook listeners, many of whom share their opinions of what they have read or heard. This community may be one with which your company wishes to engage by paying attention to what people are saying about your audiobooks. When I stopped by the site and did a search of the groups on Goodreads, I found one dedicated to audiobooks with more than eight thousand members. And that was just one group! An area of the site's pages allows publishers to announce new titles in a section called, logically enough, "Announce New Work." As we discussed with social media, don't just talk about your own publications all the time. The audiobook group has safeguarded against such behavior by limiting publishers to announcing four titles monthly. To gain a heartfelt welcome from a group, interact with the members respectfully. Give respect and get respect.

You can get more than publicity from Goodreads and the other audiobook fan and audiobook professional communities online. You can also learn a great deal. There are things I learn by seeing what others post. Think of how much knowledge is available by watching and reading and even posting when it's germane.

The main thing to remember about any of the interactive communities is that they each have protocols. If you violate the protocols, you may find yourself banned from the group. One of the first things to do when engaging with a new community is to learn its rules.

What If You Get a Bad Review?

Here is a life lesson: Poor reviews do happen, and it is important to keep perspective. It doesn't help you or your audiobook to get angry or upset about it. Reviews are inherently subjective and what you think is a great audiobook or a great narrator may not seem so to whomever has been given your project to review. You are human, so it is understandable that you will be unhappy that your work is not lauded, but it happens to everyone. Sometimes reviews are good. Sometimes they are bad. Just roll with it as best you are able. It is disappointing, to be sure, but we have all been there, and we have all survived bad reviews.

There remains the potential for some good to come out of receiving a bad review. If you can get past your initial reaction, read it again to see if there is anything helpful in it. This isn't just me being Pollyanna and seeing the good in everything. Sometimes we grow stronger from the things that hurt us. That's trite, isn't it? But that doesn't make it less true. For example, does the reviewer offer specifics as to what he didn't like? If so, see if the criticism rings true to you and whether it may be something you can work around in the future. Was it the content, the writing style? Or was it the narrator? Was it the quality of the recording? You may not agree with all of the comments, but you may as well see if there is any pearl of wisdom in with the grit.

Audiobook Bestseller Lists

The *New York Times* has added a monthly audiobooks best-seller list, with fifteen fiction and fifteen nonfiction listings. It includes the publisher, the number of weeks or months on the chart, whether the audiobook is on its way up or down the list, the running time of the audiobook, and the narrator's name. The newspaper's website, at www.nytimes.com, says, "Audiobook rankings are created from sales of physical and digital audio products. Free-trial or low-cost audiobook sales are not eligible for inclusion. Publisher credits for audiobooks are listed under the audiobook publisher name." *New York Times* best-seller lists are collated from reporting stores. The thousands of venues contributing information report their sales on a confidential basis, the newspaper's website says.

Publishers Weekly, a magazine we have already talked about, has an audiobook best-seller list of ten titles. It garners its data from DecisionKey (formerly BookScan) to determine sales figures and, as a bonus, it publishes those sales figures so you can indulge your curiosity as to how many copies a best-selling book sells, at least for those on the current lists. Interestingly, the same title can appear on the list in more than one place if it is sold in different configurations.

Audible has a best-seller list, based on its own transactions, of course. We noted that Audible is owned by Amazon and has a large customer base for downloadable audiobooks, so their lists are also a good source of information to see what is selling well.

Google shows its top one hundred audiobooks in its Google Play store. The URL for that is https://play.google.com/store/books/top/category/audiobooks.

These lists are a good way to become familiar with the best-seller list landscape. Use a search engine and put in the phrase "audiobook best-seller lists," and you will likely find even more of them.

JESSICA'S SIXTH RULE OF AUDIOBOOK PUBLISHING

As a reward for getting this far through the book, here is my bonus Sixth Rule of Audiobook Publishing: *There is no such thing as an audiobook emergency.*

What could I possibly mean by that? Of course there are audiobook emergencies. The narrator is sick or has dropped out of the project altogether; the rightsholder claims they never agreed to terms and won't send back a signed agreement; a customer is waiting for a big order and the project is late; the studio you booked, sight unseen, is unusable; the editor did a poor job and you need to find a new editor, stat!

Yes, these are all problems with the project, some of which are insurmountable. Any of these can cause you to have a bad day, a bad week, maybe even a bad month, but they are the same types of business problems faced by myriad companies. Every business confronts adversity. I don't mean to trivialize the impact these can have on your fiscal and emotional well-being. I mean that the world will not be shaken if an audiobook is published late or not at all. Lives are not at stake. More than that, what I really mean is that this can be a useful mantra to help keep you calm when you run into obstacles. There is no such thing as an audiobook emergency.

SUMMARY

This chapter was another big serving of information. You learned about taking an audiobook to market and about marketing. You heard about tie-ins to the public's awareness, what your distributor will need from you, discount rates to retailers, awards and reviews, best-seller lists. You heard from Jorjeana Marie and Karen Commins with advice about building a platform and how to make your audiobook visible to consumers. As a bonus, now you know my Fifth Rule for Audiobook Publishers, that it is the publisher's responsibility to market their audiobooks, and the Sixth Rule for Audiobook Publishers, that there are no audiobook emergencies. Now for a heaping spoonful of more legal stuff.

CHAPTER 10

More Legal Stuff

Everyone who runs a business needs to know about the laws that have an impact on that industry. Those who are in the business of audiobooks are no exception. We have already discussed some legal issues, such as contracts and copyrights, but there is more for you to know. Let's jump right in.

BUSINESS FORMATS

First, let's look at the various types of business formats there are and which one may make the most sense for you. As my clients all know, or should know by now, I am always in favor of forming either a corporation or an LLC, which stands for Limited Liability Company. It is called that because, similar to a corporation, it shields its members from being personally liable for any liability of the company. For example, if the company gets in debt to a vendor, you will not owe that debt yourself if you have taken steps to incorporate or to form an LLC. The exception to this is if you have signed a personal guarantee, which can make you personally liable for obligations of your company.

I cannot address the types or requirements of LLCs in other states, but it is a favored form of business here in California because it is easy to form, it doesn't have the requirements of corporations in regard to having to keep minutes, having shares and shareholders, and so on, even if that corporation has just one or two people. An LLC has a simple formation document, and along with the LLC but not provided by the state, you should have an Operating Agreement. The Operating Agreement will set out the number of members you can have in the LLC (note: LLCs have members, not shareholders) and how the company is to be governed, which tends to be particularly important in regard to how to handle one or more members leaving the LLC. This can be simple or complicated, it can be a buyout by the other members, or it can cause the business to shut down. How your company operates (that is why it is called an Operating Agreement) is up to you. There are some basic terms and it is relatively easy to find an operating agreement you should be able to live with.

In some states, including California, you can form what is called a single member LLC. You still get the same protections from personal liability that you would with multiple members. The difference is that the IRS will disregard the LLC for purposes of tax liability and view it as personal income to you. In fact, they call it a disregarded entity. It is only disregarded by the IRS. Your liability protections remain.

This discussion is just to give you an idea of what an LLC is. This is not going to be a treatise on LLCs or what format you should choose. Discuss that with your attorney and your CPA to determine what is best for you. They may suggest a partnership, a DBA, or a corporation.

FIRST SALE DOCTRINE

The next bit of legal stuff is about the First Sale Doctrine. I told you in Chapter 2 that the Doctrine allows you to sell or lend a copyrighted item that you have legally purchased. On its website, the United States Department of Justice discusses the First Sale Doctrine. The government has posted, in part, the following:

> The first sale doctrine, codified at 17 U.S.C. § 109, provides that
> an individual who knowingly purchases a copy of a copyrighted

work from the copyright holder receives the right to sell, display, or otherwise dispose of *that particular copy*, notwithstanding the interests of the copyright owner. The right to distribute ends, however, once the owner has sold *that particular copy*. ... Since the first sale doctrine never protects a defendant who makes unauthorized reproductions of a copyrighted work, the first sale doctrine cannot be a successful defense in cases that allege infringing reproduction.

Further, the privileges created by the first sale principle do not "extend to any person who has acquired possession of the copy or phonorecord from the copyright owner, by rental, lease, loan, or otherwise, without acquiring ownership of it." *See* 17 U.S.C. § 109(d).

If you would like to read more about this, the Web page I have quoted is, at the time of this writing, at: www.justice.gov/usam /criminal-resource-manual-1854-copyright-infringement-first -sale-doctrine.

WHEN CAN A COPYRIGHT OWNER *NOT* EXPLOIT THEIR INTELLECTUAL PROPERTY?

This sounds like the setup to an unfunny joke, but it is not a laughing matter. In Chapter 2, I told you we would talk here about an instance when the owner of a copyright in a recording cannot use it. We have already discussed it, but it bears repeating so that you don't endanger yourself or, on the flip side, you know when to assert your rights.

When the rights to an audiobook have been licensed and those rights revert (whether through expiration of term, breach of contract, or through some other means), the rightsholder once again becomes the owner, free to use or license or let lie fallow what belongs to them. In the meantime, the licensee has created a recording and, barring any contractual agreements otherwise, that licensee owns the copyright to the recording. The copyright to the recording is separate from the copyright to the underlying material, similar to the way the copyright to a translation is separate from the copyright to the underlying material.

As the license agreement has terminated, the licensee may no longer exploit the recording, whether by sale, rental, or gift. The audio publisher has lost the right to use the recording because it no longer has the right to utilize the underlying material that gave rise to the audiobook. Here is your example of someone who owns the copyright to intellectual property, the audiobook recording, but does not have the legal right to use it.

This is important to you as an audiobook publisher so you are aware that when your license to material expires, you may no longer publish your audiobook. There are many exceptions to that exception, though. For example, your licensing agreement should have a sell-off clause if you are planning to publish hard copies. That sell-off period means that after the term of the agreement expires, you still have a specified amount of time in which to get rid of your inventory by selling it, whether back to the licensor or to third parties such as remainder buyers. Of course, if you and the licensor agree to extend your contract term, then you will be able to continue to sell the audiobook.

If you *are* the licensor, then when the license agreement expires and the rights revert to you, if you see the audiobook being sold or rented or otherwise out in the world, unless you have agreed to allow it, the publisher of the audiobook is infringing on your rights (if it is the audiobook publisher who has made the product available post-expiration). If it is a reseller, then there is no infringement. Remember the First Sale Doctrine from Chapter 2 and earlier in this chapter.

PUBLIC DOMAIN

I have told you that something that is in the public domain is not protected by copyright. It may be something that was once copyrighted but is no longer protected by it, or perhaps was never protected by copyright in the first place, such as a U.S. government-issued document. This latter category explains why there are multiple audio versions of the same material. Examples include the United States Constitution and the Declaration of Independence, two government documents in the public domain. If you noted to yourself that they would be public domain anyway because of their age, you get bonus points! A more contemporary example would be the Constitutional Amendments because some were enacted in the latter part of the twentieth century.

How do you know if a book is still protected by copyright? That gets a little bit tricky because the copyright statutes have changed over time, providing different measuring sticks for books written during different eras.

Another U.S. government website, the Copyright Office, provides an explanation about the life of a copyright:

> In general, for works created on or after January 1, 1978, the term of copyright is the life of the author plus seventy years after the author's death. If the work is a joint work with multiple authors, the term lasts for seventy years after the last surviving author's death. For works made for hire and anonymous or pseudonymous works, the duration of copyright is 95 years from publication or 120 years from creation, whichever is shorter. For works created before January 1, 1978, that were not published or registered as of that date, the term of copyright is generally the same as for works created on or after January 1, 1978. The law, however, provides that in no case would the term have expired before December 31, 2002, and if the work was published on or before that date, the term will not expire

before December 31, 2047. For works created before January 1, 1978, that were published or registered before that date, the initial term of copyright was twenty-eight years from the date of publication with notice or from the date of registration. At the end of the initial term, the copyright could be renewed for another sixty-seven years for a total term of protection of up to ninety-five years. To extend copyright into the renewal term, two registrations had to be made before the original term expired: one for the original term and the other for the renewal term. This requirement was eliminated on June 26, 1992, and renewal term registration is now optional.

Determining whether or not something is still under copyright can be confusing. If you need assistance, contact an attorney with expertise in copyright law to help unravel and sort the issue. Prior to that, or if you cannot find an attorney to help you, what I always recommend when you want to do an audiobook version and you're unsure whether the book is in the public domain, is to contact the publisher. And you should probably always have doubt, unless it is really quite old. It is always better to be safe than sorry because people are not amused when their copyrights are violated. And if the book has a registered copyright and it was done in a timely fashion, then the penalty is possibly very costly. There are statutory penalties that can be sought by the rightsholder.

That is why I suggest that you start with the publisher, especially if it's one of the big publishers. They may not have thorough files going back to early twentieth century or even mid-twentieth century, but for the most part, they can find contracts. You just have to give them time. If they can't determine the copyright status from their own files, they will tell you. Sometimes you have to figure it out in other ways. The United States Copyright Office does have records online, but they are not comprehensive. They have information for copyrights issued from January 1, 1978, to the present. Anything prior to 1978 would require a search of the U.S. Copyright Office records. There are companies that will do those searches, for a fee, and the Copyright Office will also do those searches for a fee. You can even do the search yourself, in person at the U.S. Copyright Office at the Library of Congress in Washington, DC.

Cornell University's website has a thorough chart that lists different types of intellectual property and how to determine the date when something enters the public domain, if you have some basic information, such as whether the book was published or unpublished and, if published, the initial publication date and whether or not the copyright was ever registered. That chart is located at https://copyright.cornell .edu/sites/default/files/2018-01/copyright_term_and_the_public _domain2018.pdf.

Note: Just because something is in the public domain in the United States does not mean it is public domain in other countries, such as the United Kingdom. This is because copyright laws differ country to country. If you are able to have someone knowledgeable help you figure out whether a book is in the public domain worldwide, great. Then you can release it worldwide. You can release it worldwide anyway if you are sure that it is in the public domain everywhere, but be aware that you may get a smackdown if someone abroad discovers or believes that you are infringing their copyright. This has happened to clients of mine who filled out metadata forms stating they held worldwide rights. When those rights were challenged in a particular territory by another publisher, it turned out the client's rights were actually limited to the specific territories in which the title was in the public domain or to which a contract had been negotiated. Bye-bye, worldwide sales.

Also important to know is that although a book may be in the public domain in the language in which it was originally written, a translation of the book may still be protected by copyright. That's right, a translation of a book has its own copyright. Pick up a book by, let's say, Fyodor Dostoevsky, the famed Russian writer, open the copyright page, and look at the copyright notice for the translation. This is important to you because if the translation is copyrighted, then even though *Crime and Punishment* itself may be in the public domain, the translation you wish to use may require you to negotiate a contract with the translator. If the translation was done a very long time ago, it may also be in the public domain.

FAIR USE

Drum roll, please: the moment you have been waiting for! It's the discussion about fair use. This is not an exhaustive look at fair use, but it will give you some insight into what the doctrine of fair use means and what it means for you. Spoiler alert: For you, as a commercial publisher, it means do not use copyrighted materials without the express written permission of the rightsholder.

Fair use is oft cited by those using quotes without permission, whether from books, music, film clips, you name it. If it is copyrighted, there is probably someone who has decided it is okay to use it because of the unicorn known as fair use. Yes, that is hyperbole, but my point is that many people use the phrase fair use as though it entitles them to anything they like, so long as they follow whatever rule they heard from someone else.

Fair use isn't a unicorn, though. It is real, and here is the very important thing you need to know: Fair use is not a right. Fair use is a defense against a claim of copyright infringement.

What does "it's not a right, it's a defense" mean to you?

Here is what the U.S. Copyright Office has to say in a very brief blurb.

Under the fair use doctrine of the U.S. copyright statute, it is permissible to use limited portions of a work including quotes, for purposes such as commentary, criticism, news reporting, and scholarly reports. There are no legal rules permitting the use of a specific number of words, a certain number of musical notes, or percentage of a work. Whether a particular use qualifies as fair use depends on all the circumstances.

It is a little bit tricky to anticipate what will or will not be considered fair use. As it is a defense and not a right (feel free to make this another mantra so that you remain mindful of it), then if you use someone else's copyrighted material without obtaining their permission, you will not know whether you have used it in a manner permissible under the law until a judge or jury delivers a verdict in a case brought against you for copyright infringement. This is what it means to say that fair use is a defense. Someone sues you for copyright infringement, you claim the use was fair use and the court agrees with you. Phew! Or, alternatively, someone sues you for copyright infringement, you claim fair use as a defense and the court disagrees. Not phew.

Take a look at the language used in the quote from the Copyright Office. If you break down its meaning, you see it says you may use part of someone else's copyrighted work without a license from them in certain circumstances. Those uses include commentary, criticism, news reporting, and scholarly reports. The Copyright Office even addresses some of the old wives' tales about fair use when it says there is no specific number of notes of a song you can use, no specific number of words or percentage of a work. Many of you have heard these tropes and have believed them, or wanted to believe them. Believe the U.S. Copyright Office when it says these are not true.

There is just one takeaway from this as it affects you as an audiobook publisher: Do not publish anything copyrighted by someone else without a license from them granting permission to do so. You are conducting a commercial enterprise, putting your audiobooks into the marketplace for purposes of commerce. You want to sell them. You want to receive revenue in exchange for them. That is not a protected fair use of someone else's work.

There may be circumstances in which fair use will be a viable defense for you, but why risk it? Always, always, always, get permission when possible. If it isn't possible, don't use someone else's copyrighted material.

Got it? Good.

DMCA, THE DIGITAL MILLENNIUM COPYRIGHT ACT

The Digital Millennium Copyright Act (DMCA) of 1998 is another law you ought to know something about, not only if you are going to have a website that hosts content but also because it may govern how you get your pirated audiobooks removed from law-abiding websites. I am only going to focus on one part of the DMCA and that is how to give notice to websites that are hosting your audiobooks without your permission.

The DMCA is, in part, a portion of the copyright law that outlines take-down procedures. If you find your materials on a website and you are certain you did not authorize that site to carry your audiobooks, then under the DMCA, you are entitled to give notice to have the program or programs removed from that site. This is something the site itself does; there is no entity that comes in and does it for them. It isn't a search and seizure, where the law removes materials that shouldn't be there. No, it falls to you to notify them that you want them to take down your intellectual property.

The DMCA has specific procedures for giving such notice. To do so, your notice must do the following.

1. Notify the Web host by sending the notice to the company's DMCA agent or to an abuse or take-down department, if there is one;
2. Provide the location of the item, including the URL and the title;
3. Include your contact information;
4. State clearly that all of the information in the take-down notice you are providing is correct;
5. State under penalty of perjury that the person sending the notice, whether that is you or your agent, has the right to act on behalf of the copyright holder;
6. The notice must be signed by you or your agent, although it can be signed either electronically or physically.

Note that the word agent as used here does not mean someone who gets you a part in a movie or sells your book to a publisher. It means someone who is designated by you to do something on your behalf; in this instance, send a take-down notice. The agent can be your attorney, someone at your workplace, your mom, or anyone else handling the task.

Some websites have their own forms and procedures for take-down notices, so use theirs and send it to wherever and whomever they instruct you to send it. A search of the website for "DMCA," "take-down notice," or "copyright infringement" should help you determine whether or not a given website has its own form.

Once you have sent your notice, the website is required to notify the person or company that posted the offending material, permitting them to challenge your take-down request.

This might result in the immediate removal of your material from the site, or there may be a long lag time. My experience with sending take-down notices on behalf of clients is that some sites are prompt to address these notices, and some are not only slow but may require repeated effort on your part to have an effect. Not all websites are based in countries that are likely to be responsive to these notices. Expect little from those sites. You may be pleasantly surprised, or you may be ignored.

As for your own website, if you allow third parties to post intellectual property, you will need a procedure for addressing take-down notices in the event any of the posted materials are or are claimed to be infringing the rights of someone other than the original poster.

GDPR

Another law recently went into effect, and in this case you need to be aware of it if you are the owner of a website that collects personal data from its visitors. This law, known as the General Data Protection Regulation (GDPR), went into effect internationally on May 25, 2018. The law's intent is to protect online privacy. It is a European Union (EU) law, but its impact has been felt globally, as it applies to all companies doing business with the European Economic Area (the EEA). For example, you may have noticed an influx of emails from websites you use or to which you subscribe, asking you to opt in to their new rules or telling you that you can opt out. Of course, you already could have opted out of receiving website communications. The point is that even U.S. sites want to be in compliance with the GDPR because, for many sites, their customer base is international. In order to be able to continue to operate without fear of violating the new privacy laws, many sites simply have complied with GDPR requirements, even though they are based in non-EU countries.

The GDPR is intended to make companies more transparent in their use of the information they collect from their online visitors.

OTHER WEBSITE PROTOCOLS YOU NEED TO KNOW ABOUT

The greater part of audiobook commerce is conducted on the internet. If you don't already have a website for your business, it is important to build one. That means knowing a bit about the laws governing online conduct.

Terms and Conditions

If you are planning to operate your own website for the sales of audiobooks, there are companies that can help you set up such a site, or maybe you have the knowledge with which to do it yourself. Regardless of who builds it, you will need to have Terms and Conditions to which users of the site must agree.

What are Terms and Conditions? When you go to a website and it asks you to check a box to indicate your agreement with their legalese, you are agreeing to their terms and conditions, which are exactly what they sound like. They are the rules set by the website's owner. Those rules govern how you and they interact, who owns anything you post or use, what the Rules of Civility are that govern the site (with appreciation to Amor Towles and George Washington).

For interactive websites, those that allow users to post opinions or content, most likely you have agreed to be polite and not harass anyone. You will likely have agreed that the website owns anything you post and that you will not violate anyone's copyright, among other things.

You want these same protections for your website, particularly, albeit not only, if you are either conducting sales from your site, allowing streaming or downloads from your site, or allowing users to interact in some way. Protect yourself and your content by having users agree to your Terms and Conditions. Do take the time and money to make sure they are tailored to the specific uses and purposes of your website. Building a business is costly but skipping protection of the business can be even more expensive. Hire an attorney experienced in this arena. You may change and adapt your Terms and Conditions as time goes on and you learn things about running your site that you did not anticipate. That is fine, it happens. Haven't you often had to agree to the new terms from companies with which you had previously clicked the "I AGREE" button? It's called evolution.

Whether it is your initial outing with your website or an update, please, please, please always use an attorney who knows how to draft these documents with specificity that is tailored to your business. It is like finding a good seamstress who knows to measure twice, cut once. Without an experienced lawyer to help you, you may not even know what protective language to include or exclude, much less what those words mean and how they offer you safeguards.

COPPA

An essential part of your legal language depends on whether your website is safe for and intended for use by children under the age of thirteen. The Children's Online Privacy Protection Act (COPPA) restricts the collection of information about website visitors younger than thirteen. According to the Federal Trade Commission's website, "[COPPA] spells out what operators of websites and online services must do to protect children's privacy and safety online. For example, if your company is covered by COPPA, you need to have certain information in your privacy policy and get parental consent before collecting some types of information from kids under thirteen."

The site goes on to say the following: "Violations can result in law enforcement actions, including civil penalties, so compliance counts."

I am not telling you this to alarm you. Rather, this is vital information for you to build your business and its outreach to customers in a way that complies with the law while offering your products. It isn't as intimidating as it may seem. All you need to do is comply.

"Easy for you to say," I can imagine you grumbling. "How do I even know what to do to comply?"

Sometimes Uncle Sam makes things clear and accessible and in fact the Federal Trade Commission (FTC) website offers six steps to compliance with COPPA. They are:

1. Determine if your company is a website or online service that collects personal information from kids under thirteen.
2. Post a privacy policy that complies with COPPA.
3. Notify parents directly before collecting personal information from their kids.
4. Get parents' verifiable consent before collecting personal information from their kids.
5. Honor parents' ongoing rights with respect to personal information collected from their kids.
6. Implement reasonable procedures to protect the security of kids' personal information.

Each of these steps is covered in detail with a link to a complete description on the FTC website at www.ftc.gov/tips-advice/business -center/guidance/childrens-online-privacy-protection-rule-six -step-compliance. If you need to look them up and don't have this book at hand, just do a Web search for "COPPA FTC steps" and you should be able to find it easily. In addition, the FTC website also has an FAQ.

In summary, if you may have visitors under age thirteen, compliance with federal law in structuring your website is extremely important. Use web developers and attorneys with expertise in these arenas so that you don't get hurt and, more important, you have complied with the law to help keep minors safe during their time on your website.

You don't think your site can possibly harm anyone, I know. That's good, it means you don't think like a predator. Predators think like predators. That's why these laws exist.

SUMMARY

Though the initial chapters were full of legal information, you discovered that there was much more to know. In this chapter, you were introduced to the business formats of corporations and LLCs, which offer protection of your personal assets in the event of business liability. You can now contemplate which business format may be best for you. You learned about the First Sale Doctrine, and you heard an exception to a copyright owner's ability to use his own intellectual property. There was a discussion of public domain and fair use, of the DMCA take-down procedures and the GDPR. You now know that your own website will need Terms and Conditions and that there are international laws which are relevant to you. You have learned of necessary steps to protect the under-13 age group. This is another chapter you may want to refer back to as you formulate your business and your business practices.

AFTERWORD

If you have made it all the way through this book, you have learned a lot about producing and publishing audiobooks. You also likely have a number of questions. Keep a list of those questions. If you want to ask me anything, you can tweet me at @jessicakayeesq or you can email me at jessica@bighappyfamilyaudio.com. I may not be able to answer every question, but I will try to respond to as many as I can. Please note that by asking, you may find your question posted on my websites, along with my answer.

Audiobooks are subject to changes in technology as much as any other media format. Some of the advice you have learned may change because of technological changes. Much of the advice is—dare I say it—sound and will remain sound regardless of how audiobooks are delivered to the consumer in the future.

The audiobook community has grown tremendously over the past two decades. It is a community of people who, for the most part, are enthusiastic and painstaking about their work. The growth has been fueled by opportunity but also by the creation of good audiobooks. As you begin or continue your work in this field, please keep in mind the goal of contributing not just recordings but quality recordings.

It is a fun industry, it can be a profitable industry, and it is a collegial industry. Welcome to the fold.

Blog Post About Directing a Grammy-Winning Audiobook

In 2018, Carrie Fisher posthumously won the Grammy Award for Best Spoken Recording for her audiobook version of her last book, *The Princess Diarist*. I was Carrie's director and subsequent to *The Princess Diarist* winning the Grammy, I was asked to write a blog post about the experience of directing the winning program. That blog post was featured both by Penguin Random House, the publisher of *The Princess Diarist* in both book and audiobook formats, and the publisher of this book, F+W Media, Inc., on their respective websites. That blog post appears here.

THE MAKING OF A GRAMMY-WINNING AUDIOBOOK: DIRECTING AN ICON

What makes a Grammy Award–winning audiobook? A look at the past winners reveals there is a wide spectrum of answers to that question. It has to do with good writing, with good narration, at times it has to do with popularity and with timeliness. There is no one recipe for a winning audiobook, but I can tell you the ingredients that helped make *The Princess Diarist* by Carrie Fisher the 2018 winner of the Grammy Award for Best Spoken Word.

In October of 2016, Carrie Fisher was in a recording studio to narrate her soon-to-be-released memoir, *The Princess Diarist*, for her publisher, Penguin Random House Audio. The book is a charming portrait of the person she was in the twenty-first century versus the also charming, much more naïve young lady of nineteen, who starred as Princess Leia in Star Wars. On January 28, 2018, *The Princess Diarist* and Carrie Fisher won the Grammy Award for Best Spoken Album.

The genesis of *The Princess Diarist* was that Carrie found a journal she had kept during the making of the first Star Wars film. Her writing as a teenager was strikingly incisive and clear, a harbinger of the great writer she was to become. From the fortuitous discovery of forty-year-old notes came *The Princess Diarist*. In it, she revealed a long-kept secret but, more than that, produced a moving and powerful work, juxtaposing the current Carrie against who she had been, a subject that touches all of us who are fortunate enough to live long enough to reminisce.

Carrie's book became all the more poignant when she died at age sixty, just a few weeks after she and her daughter, Billie Lourd, finished recording the audiobook. Carrie wanted her daughter to record the journal entries, since Billie was close to the age Carrie had been when she wrote those notes.

And who am I to write about Carrie and her work? I was her audiobook director for *The Princess Diarist*. Thanks to Penguin Random House Audio producer Dan Zitt, I was hired to be the very fortunate woman on the other side of the glass from Carrie. It was my job to tell her when she misread something, or when there was a noise and we needed to do a retake; to take notes for her if she found an error in the manuscript; to go over her calendar to figure out when we could meet for another recording session; or to tell her that lunch had arrived.

I can anticipate your first question. Yes, Gary Fisher, Carrie's dog, was at the studio for each session. Yes, he is adorable and yes, he adored her.

Working with a celebrity is much like working with anyone, in terms of getting an audiobook recorded. They narrate the words while the computer records their voice. Working with some-one who is recording their memoir, however, is special because it requires inherent respect for the narrator as the creator of the words as well as their delivery. Do you correct someone when they are reading their own work but they say something for which you believe the inflection is incorrect? Well, yes, you do. That is a part of the director's responsibilities.

Carrie was easy to work with. She took comments and sugges-tions well. But directors don't treat the process as a dictatorship. It is a collaboration. She and I had conversations about why some-thing may or may not work or whether something easily suscepti-ble to interpretation when read needed a different sort of specific-ity when spoken aloud. Being a good audiobook director takes an ear for language and cadence and grammar, and an eye kept on the printed page at nearly all times to ensure a close match of the audio to the text. Yet, sometimes all of those things are thrown out the window and all that matters is what the author wants, especially if it well serves the project.

But Carrie was a dream to work with. She engaged with ques-tions or suggestions, some from her and some from me. She was fun and whip-smart and personable and, considering I knew her for just a few days, I was completely in awe of her and smitten. The ingredients that made this audiobook a winner were two parts Carrie Fisher, one part Billie Lourd, and 100 percent alluring writ-ing and performances.

Audiobook
Publication Contract

Note: Many publishers will have their own contract that they prefer to use, but if you are asked to provide a contract, this is a skeleton of some of the key clauses you need. Please be aware there are nuances in every deal—and so this is not necessarily a one-contract-fits-all situation. With that in mind, here are some basic clauses with which you should become familiar.

This will confirm the agreement made between Publisher *[fill in your company name and address here]* (hereinafter "Publisher"), and *[fill in other company or person's name and address here]*, (hereinafter "Rightsholder"), concerning a work entitled _____ _____*[put name of book here]* (hereinafter "Work"), written by _____*[put author's name here]*, in which Rightsholder is the sole and exclusive owner of all Rights, as hereinafter defined.

1. Rights:

    The Rightsholder hereby grants Publisher the sole and exclusive worldwide audio rights for the term of ten (10) *[Note: It could be any term and is typically five, seven, or ten years.]* years beginning on the date of publication of the audiobook contemplated hereunder, to publish unabridged recordings of the Work, to edit and revise and adapt the Work, and to record electronically, or in any other manner now known or hereafter developed, the Work for the purpose of duplication and distribution in any forms now known or hereafter developed (hereinafter "Audiobook") and to sell, license and distribute the Audiobook under the Publisher's label or its assigns. Also granted is permission to use the Rightsholder's and author's names in advertisement, publicity and/or promotion of the Audiobook, provided that the Rightsholder's and author's names will not be used in any endorsement or testimonial without Rightsholder's prior written consent, which consent shall not be unreasonably withheld. All such rights shall hereinafter be referred to as "Rights." Rightsholder shall not receive any additional compensation for such endorsement or testimonial. All other rights including but not limited to print, motion picture, and television, remain with the Rightsholder.

2. Royalties:

As consideration for any and all rights in the Work granted by Rightsholder hereunder, Publisher shall pay Rightsholder as follows:

(a) On sales of the Audiobook, less returns of unsold stock: Eight percent (8%) of net wholesale income received. Catalog, book, record or tape club and foreign sales payable at fifty percent (50%) of regular royalty rate. *[Note: The 8 percent may be low in today's market. You may see 10, 12, or even 15 percent on hard copy sales, if you are doing hard copy. Resist 15 percent.]*

(b) On revenue received for downloads of the Audiobook, fifteen percent (15%) of net wholesale income received. *[Note: Fifteen percent is fine for download sales. It can go up to 50 percent but should not exceed 50 percent unless you are working with a best-selling title—and even then, only if it is hugely best-selling.]*

(c) On use of the Audiobooks for review, advertising, publicity or the like to promote the sale and distribution of the Audiobook, no royalties shall be paid. No royalties shall be paid on any Audiobooks sold to Rightsholder at a discount, given in exchange for damaged or defective goods or for sales of remainders or overstocks.

3. Accounting:

Publisher agrees to render an accounting to Rightsholder, which shall cover the period to the thirty-first day of December or the thirtieth day of June, whichever first follows publication of the Audiobook, then semi-annually during the first two (2) years following release of Audiobook by Publisher. After the initial two (2) year period, Publisher shall render a statement annually if sales in any calendar year period total a minimum of one hundred (100) copies, whereafter Publisher shall only render statements annually after each period where the total number of units sold for the preceding period(s) exceed one hundred (100) copies. Publisher shall send such statements, with checks in payment of amounts due, on or about the last day of March and September. Publisher shall maintain a reasonable reserve, not to exceed twenty-five percent (25%), against returns of the Audiobook and the amount thereof shall be deducted from the payments to Rightsholder. Rightsholder shall have the right to inspect Publisher's books of accounting, upon reasonable written request and sufficient notice, to determine the accuracy of statements rendered to Rightsholder, provided that there may not be more than one such examination in any twelve-month period, and that each such statement shall be deemed incontestable two years after the date upon which such statement is issued unless an examination has taken place and a claim with respect thereto has been asserted in such two-year period.

4. Warranty:

The Rightsholder warrants and represents that the Work is original; that Rightsholder is the sole author and proprietor of the Work or is otherwise legally entitled to enter into this Agreement; that Rightsholder has the full power and authority to enter into this agreement and to grant the Rights granted hereunder to Publisher; that there are no claims, liens or encumbrances against the Work, that Rightsholder has not previously assigned, transferred or otherwise encumbered the Work in any manner which will conflict, interfere with, or impair the Rights granted to Publisher herein. Rightsholder further warrants and represents that the Work, when published by Publisher, will not infringe upon any statutory or common law, invade the right of privacy or publicity of any third person, or contain any matter that is defamatory, libelous or slanderous or otherwise in contravention of the rights of any third persons or party anywhere in the world, that nothing contained in the Work is injurious, harmful or damaging to the health of a user, and that all statements in the Work asserted as facts are true or are based upon reasonable research for accuracy. Rightsholder agrees to indemnify and hold harmless Publisher, and its officers, directors, shareholders, employees, agents, representatives, successors, licensees, assigns, distributors and any seller of the CD against any loss, liability, damage, cost, expense, claim, demand, action or proceeding that may be brought, including reasonable attorney fees and costs, arising from a breach or alleged breach of warranties set forth in this paragraph or otherwise arising from the Work or the Rights thereto. *[Indemnification is in the event someone sues you for something the rightsholder has warranted is okay for you to do. Note that indemnification is helpful if your rightsholder has deep pockets but otherwise may be fairly meaningless if they do not have the money or insurance coverage to actually indemnify you.]*

5. Rightsholder's Copies:

Publisher shall give the Rightsholder, free of charge, five (5) *[Note: Give as many copies as you wish. Five is not a hard and fast rule.]* copies of the Audiobook. If published in hard copy, should the Rightsholder desire more copies, Publisher will provide the same at a discount of fifty percent (50%) from retail, with no royalties paid on such sales.

6. Assignment:

The provisions of this Agreement shall apply to, inure to the benefit of and bind the heirs, successors, executors, administrators, and assigns of the Rightsholder, and the successors and assigns of Publisher.

7. Copyright:

Publisher shall copyright the Audiobook and shall own the copyright thereto. *[Note: The rightsholder keeps the copyright to the underlying material. You, the publisher, will own the copyright only to the audio recording and when your term expires, absent an agreement otherwise, you will no longer have the right to exploit the recording, even if you own the copyright to it.]*

8. Remedies:

Rightsholder agrees that no default by Publisher shall cause Rightsholder irreparable damage entitling Rightsholder to an injunction or other equitable relief; it being agreed that Rightsholder shall be entitled to seek only monetary damages, if any, for a default by Publisher hereunder.

9. Arbitration:

Any controversy arising under any provision of this Agreement shall first be attempted to be settled by mediation. In the event mediation cannot settle the controversy, the matter shall be settled by arbitration in Los Angeles, California, by the American Arbitration Association under its rules as in effect on the date of delivery of demand for arbitration. Any award resolved thereunder may be confirmed by the Superior Court of the State of California, County of Los Angeles. This Agreement shall be interpreted according to the laws of the State of California and the United States. *[Note: Substitute any state you are in. The rightsholder may require their state instead. Whether to give in depends on how important it is to you and whether it is worth it to argue about it. You will not win with one of the big publishers in regard to where to arbitrate or bring suit. They will insist that the contract state their preference, not yours.]*

10. <u>Integration</u>:

This Agreement contains the entire understanding of the parties, and may not be modified, nor shall any waiver be effective, unless in writing and signed by all the parties.

AGREED TO AND ACCEPTED:

By: _____ By:_____

Its: _____ Its: _____

[Note: The line above means the person's title at the company , e.g., President, Owner, Managing Member, etc.]

DATED: _____ DATED: _____

Narration Agreement

This Narration Agreement is entered into by and between _____ _____ (Narrator), with the address of _____ _____ and _____, (Publisher or Producer), with the address of _____.

1. Narrator agrees to perform narration on a sound recording (the Work) entitled: _____ on such dates and at such times as shall be mutually agreeable. *[Alternative clause: The recording shall be concluded by _____ (insert date.)]*

   [Note: If the narrator is to record at home, add how the audio files are to be delivered, add what format they are to be in, add whether they are to be delivered edited or unedited or partially edited, à la punch and roll recording.]

2. As full and complete consideration for any and all services performed and rights granted to Producer by Narrator hereunder, Producer shall pay Narrator the sum of _____ *[insert flat fee amount or, if royalty only, the royalty amount or if per finished hour amount then the amount Per Finished Hour (PFH) or if any combination, then set forth each part of the compensation]* upon Narrator's completion of the Work in a manner satisfactory to Publisher (or Producer), inclusive of returning to the studio to record pickups, as necessary.

3. Publisher (or Producer) shall have the exclusive and perpetual right, throughout the universe, to publish and distribute, and/ or cause or authorize third parties to publish and distribute, reproductions of the Work in any form now known or hereafter devised, including but not limited to whether physical, e.g., CDs, or incorporeal reproduction, e.g., digital downloads. The format in which the Work is to be produced and distributed,

the manner of distribution, the nature and extent of advertising and promotion, pricing and discount schedules and packaging, if any, to be used shall be in Publisher's (or Producer's) sole discretion. Nothing herein shall be deemed to obligate Publisher (or Producer) to use or otherwise exploit the Work.

4. Narrator hereby grants and assigns to Publisher (or Producer), exclusively and in perpetuity, all rights, whether currently existing or hereafter existing, in and to the results and proceeds of Narrator's services and performances pursuant to this Agreement and any and all material, writings, ideas or dialogue composed, submitted or interpolated by Narrator in connection with the preparation or production of the Work. All said materials, and any copyrights therein, shall automatically become the property of the Publisher (or Producer), which shall be the author thereof, it being agreed and acknowledged that all of the said materials are a work specially ordered or commissioned for use as a part of the Work and constitute a work made for hire within the meaning of the Copyright Laws of the United States, or any similar laws throughout the world. In the event the Work is found not to be a Work for Hire, Narrator hereby assigns any and all copyright in the Work to Publisher. For the avoidance of confusion, Narrator shall sign the Assignment of Copyright attached to this Agreement.

5. Narrator warrants that he/she is free to enter into this Agreement and to perform in accordance with its terms.

6. Publisher (or Producer) shall have the right to use the name and likeness of, and biographical information concerning Narrator on the Work and the packaging thereof, if any, including any digitally transmitted information and any and all advertising, publicity and/or promotion relating thereto.

7. Narrator shall not perform on other recordings of the text of the Work, or any excerpts therefrom, without Publisher's (or

Producer's) prior written permission. Narrator may perform in motion pictures, television programs or any other dramatizations of the Work and its underlying text.

8. This Agreement shall be binding upon and inure to the benefit of the parties and their respective successors, assigns and licensees.

9. If any provision of this Agreement shall be found to be void, invalid or unenforceable, the same shall in no way affect any other provision of this Agreement, the application of any such provision in any other circumstance, or the validity or enforceability of this Agreement.

10. This Agreement contains the entire understanding of the parties hereto and may not be modified, nor shall any waiver be effective, unless in writing and signed by all the parties hereto.

11. The parties agree that if any legal action is necessary to enforce this Agreement, the prevailing party shall be entitled to reasonable attorneys' fees in addition to any other relief to which that party may be entitled.

AGREED AND ACCEPTED:

By: _____ By: _____

Narrator (type in name)   Publisher (or Producer) (type in name)

DATE: _____ DATE: _____

COPYRIGHT ASSIGNMENT

FOR GOOD AND VALUABLE CONSIDERATION, receipt of which is hereby acknowledged, _____ (Assignor) does hereby irrevocably transfer and assign to _____ (Assignee) and its successors and assigns, in perpetuity, all right (whether now known or hereinafter invented or discovered), title and interest, throughout the world, including any copyrights and renewals or extensions thereto, which s/he may have in the Audiobook recording (hereinafter "Audiobook") now titled ____ _____.

This assignment shall include all components of the Audiobook, together with all copyrights and any and all other rights therein and thereto throughout the world, under any law, statute, treaty or regulation heretofore known or hereafter existing, for the use of the Audiobook or infringement of the copyrights therein or any other legal or equitable right to the use and ownership thereof in any and all fields of use known or hereafter existing throughout the world and otherwise throughout the universe by any means or technology now known or hereafter existing.

Dated this _____ day of _____, 20____.

_____
Assignor

AGREED TO:

_____
Assignee

Alternate Narration Agreement

This AGREEMENT is made as of this ___ of _____,
between _____ (the "Publisher") and _____
_____, ("Narrator") concerning an audiobook currently
titled _____ (the "Audiobook").

IN consideration of the mutual promises set forth below, the
parties hereby agree as follows:

1. **AUDIO PRODUCTION**

    A. Publisher engages Narrator to record the Audiobook.

    B. Narrator shall deliver a complete recording with edited
files or raw files to be edited by Publisher, at Publisher's choice
and direction, to Publisher by a date to be mutually agreed.

2. **PRODUCTION SERVICES**

    A. Publisher shall pay Narrator as follows: *(choose one)* the
sum of _____ dollars ($) per finished hour or a flat
rate of _____ ($). Payment shall be made
upon Publisher's timely receipt of the finished and approved
Audiobook.

    B. Within thirty (30) days of receipt of Publisher's approv-
al of the completed Audiobook, Publisher shall pay Narrator.

3. **PUBLISHER APPROVALS**

    Publisher and Narrator will work in good faith to ensure
approval of the completed Audiobook. Narrator will make up
to two (2) sets of revisions of the initial 15-minute sample (the
"Sample") and up to two (2) sets of revisions of the completed Audiobook. For the Sample, Publisher will have ten (10)

business days from receipt to approve or request revisions by Narrator. Publisher will have twenty (20) business days to approve the completed Audiobook and the Narrator will have ten (10) business days to resubmit revisions, if necessary. If changes to either the initial Audiobook sample or completed Audiobook are required, Publisher shall provide detailed information and requests for changes and revisions to the Narrator. The Narrator will make revisions based on Publisher's information and submit revised versions. If, after two (2) revisions of a completed Audiobook, the Publisher does not approve the Audiobook, then Publisher may terminate this Agreement.

4. **OWNERSHIP**

Publisher shall retain all right, title, and interest in and to the Audiobook, including the copyright in the Audiobook. For the avoidance of any confusion as to copyright ownership, Narrator shall sign the Assignment of Copyright attached to this Agreement.

5. **REPRESENTATIONS, WARRANTIES, AND INDEMNITIES**

A. Each party represents and warrants to the other that it has the right to enter into this Agreement and to perform its services hereunder. Each party agrees to defend, indemnify and hold the other harmless against any loss, expense (including reasonable attorneys' fees) or damage occasioned by any claim, action, proceeding or recovery arising out of a claim which would, if sustained be in breach of any of the foregoing representations or warranties, subject to the condition that (i) a party promptly notify the other party of any such Claim; (ii) either party permit the other to defend and, at the option of the party paying the cost of the claim, action proceeding or recovery arising out of a claim, settle, at that party's expense, such Claim; and (iii) that either party provide all reasonable assistance requested by the other in connection with such Claim at the requesting party's expense.

B. The mutual representations, warranties and indemnities made herein shall survive the termination of this Agreement.

6. NOTICES

All notices required under this Agreement shall be in writing and shall be given by certified or other receipted form of mail, or by facsimile (with printed confirmation), email (acknowledgment/acceptance of receipt required), or by hand delivery to the other party at the following addresses or such other addresses as a party may specify by notice:

To: Publisher (place name)   To: Narrator (place name)

Address: Address:

Email address:_____ Email address:_____

7. FORCE MAJEURE

It shall not be deemed a breach of this Agreement if performance is delayed or impossible due to fire, flood, war, terror attack, tornado, Act of God, or other unforeseeable circumstance that is beyond the control of the party who failed to perform.

8. ASSIGNMENTS

Publisher may assign its rights in the Agreement in whole or in part to any person, firm, or corporation, and such rights may be assigned by any assignee thereof, but no such assignment will relieve either party of any obligations under the Agreement.

9. MISCELLANEOUS

A. This Agreement shall be governed by and construed under the laws of the State of _____ applicable to agreements made and fully performed therein.

B. This Agreement may not be modified orally, contains the entire understanding between the parties concerning its subject matter, and cancels and supersedes any prior understanding between the parties.

IN WITNESS HEREOF the parties hereto have duly executed this Agreement the day and year first above written.

ACCEPTED AND AGREED:

Publisher   Narrator

By: _____   By: _____

Date: _____   Date: _____

COPYRIGHT ASSIGNMENT

FOR GOOD AND VALUABLE CONSIDERATION, receipt of which is hereby acknowledged, _____ (Assignor) does hereby irrevocably transfer and assign to _____ _____(Assignee) and its successors and assigns, in perpetuity, all right (whether now known or hereinafter invented or discovered), title and interest, throughout the world, including any copyrights and renewals or extensions thereto, which s/he may have in the Audiobook recording (hereinafter "Audiobook") now titled ____ _____.

This assignment shall include all components of the Audiobook, together with all copyrights and any and all other rights therein and thereto throughout the world, under any law, statute, treaty or regulation heretofore known or hereafter existing, for the use of the Audiobook or infringement of the copyrights therein or any other legal or equitable right to the use and ownership thereof in any and all fields of use known or hereafter existing throughout the world and otherwise throughout the universe by any means or technology now known or hereafter existing.

Dated this _____ day of _____, 20____.

_____

Assignor

AGREED TO:

_____

Assignee

Glossary

ACTUAL DAMAGES: Money damages awarded for the calculable amount of actual loss resulting as a result of the actions of others.

ADVANCE: Monies paid up front to license rights. Advance means advance against royalties, so until a calculation of royalties on sales is equal to or more than the advance, no additional royalties will be due. Once the advance has earned out, then additional royalties are due beyond what was paid in the advance.

AUDIOBOOK: In the 1990s, the Audio Publishers Association defined an audiobook as a spoken word recording. This definition was intended to include nonbook–based recordings. Think of the term as inclusive, rather than exclusive.

AUDIT CLAUSE: A contractual right to examine books and records to see whether accountings have been accurate.

BACK-OF-THE-ROOM SALES: Sales you or someone on your behalf makes at an event where you have been featured, typically as a speaker.

BISAC: Book Industry Standards and Communications. It promulgates a long list of categories into which book subject matters may fall.

BREACH OF CONTRACT: Failure to adhere to the terms of a contract; see also, **Default**.

BUYOUT or **FLAT FEE:** A payment to the licensor that precludes royalties.

CD REPLICATION: CD manufacturing.

CEASE AND DESIST LETTER: A letter, typically from an attorney, to an adversary of the client, informing them of the client's objection to behavior and instructing them to cease and desist their behavior.

CLASS OF CUSTOMER: Class of customers simply means where the customer fits in your discount schedule, with like customers treated alike, such as single store orders, small chain orders, large chain orders, libraries.

COPYRIGHT: The right to use intellectual property as permitted under the law.

CURE PERIOD: A cure period means the time during which someone in breach of a contract has to fix the issue.

DEFAULT: Failure to live up to the terms of the agreement. See also, **Breach**.

DEFINED TERMS: These are the terms of a contract that are defined, often, but not always, with: 1) bold type, 2) capitalization, and/or 3) parentheses and/or quotation marks. Any time you see those words in the contract, they are intended to mean the same thing they meant in the first use in the agreement.

DOLLAR ONE: The very first dollar of sales. Contextually it means royalties are to be calculated from the first monies made in commerce from an audiobook.

DRM: Digital rights management. For audiobooks, this generally is accomplished by limiting the number of devices upon which a downloaded audiobook can play. The purpose of DRM is to reduce piracy.

DROP-SHIP: The publisher ships directly to a customer, rather than the distributor fulfilling an order or orders.

EARNED OUT: Earned out means that sales have equaled or exceeded that which are needed for a royalty calculation to show monies due to the rightsholder.

EXCLUSIVE RIGHTS: Rights granted to you are not also granted to anyone else.

FAIR USE: The right to use copyrighted material without the need to obtain the rightsholder's permission.

FINISHED HOURS: Finished hours is similar to running time. It is the term used for a measurement of how narrators and/or audio editors are paid.

GIG: A job. In this book, it refers to a narration job.

GIVE POINTS: Places in the contract where you know in advance you are able to give in, to some extent.

HARD COPY: A hard copy of something means a physical copy. For an audiobook, this might be a CD or cassette. For a book, it would mean a hardcover book or a paperback.

INDEMNIFICATION: Economic protection from the other party in the event of a breach or allegation of breach of contract.

MEMORIALIZING AN AGREEMENT: This simply means putting the terms into a written contract.

METADATA: Information provided about the publisher's products to allow resellers to have pertinent data.

NONEXCLUSIVE RIGHTS: Rights that are or may be granted to more than one entity.

NOTICE PROVISION: A contract clause stating where to send any notices arising under the agreement.

ORPHAN WORKS: Orphan works means those books and other types of intellectual property for which you are unable to find the rightsholder.

OVERSTOCKS: Inventory that exceeds projected sales for any particular time period, which the publisher chooses to sell at a discounted rate. This differs from **Remainders.**

PAYMASTER: A company which non-signatories to union contracts can use to pay union talent.

POINT OF SALE: Where the audiobook is sold to a consumer.

PUBLIC DOMAIN: If something is in the public domain, it means that it is not protected by copyright and can be used by anyone.

RECOUPMENT: Recoupment means getting back what you have spent; being made whole. It is used in publishing agreements to indicate the point at which a publisher starts to calculate royalties: after recoupment of the advance.

REMAINDERS: When a publisher takes a title out of circulation, whether temporarily or permanently, the leftover inventory may be sold off at a deeply discounted price. These are called remainders, essentially because they are what remains of inventory after the publisher has decided not to continue to sell the title into the regular retail channels at the regular retail price.

RESERVE AGAINST RETURNS: A portion of royalties earned but held back by the publisher for a limited time, to apply against the author's royalty account in the event of returns.

RETURNS: Audiobooks purchased wholesale in the book trade are typically subject to being returned by the retailer, at any time and for any reason, for credit or for immediate payment, if the retailer already paid the invoice on which the returned goods were billed; or subject to the retailer's deduction of the returns from the amount they will pay you, if the invoice had not yet been paid at the time of the return.

REVERSION OF RIGHTS: Rights which were licensed but which have been returned to the licensor.

RIGHTSHOLDER: The person or entity which is legally entitled to license audiobook rights to another person or entity.

RUNNING TIME: The length of a finished audiobook.

SELL THROUGH, SELLING THROUGH: This refers to the sale from the retailer to the consumer. The audiobook has sold through, meaning it was placed in one venue, e.g. a bookstore, and was sold to the end user, the customer.

SOURCE MATERIALS, UNDERLYING MATERIALS: This refers to the intellectual property upon which your audiobook is based, such as a book.

STATUTORY DAMAGES: Damages awarded as permitted by statute.

SUBSIDIARY RIGHTS: Subsidiary rights, or sub rights, as they are often called, can include audio rights, foreign language rights, first and second serial rights (the right to license part of the book for excerpting in a newspaper or magazine), among other sub rights, and can be exploited by the publisher either by exercising the rights themselves, e.g. by publishing a paperback or audio edition of a book first published in hardcover, *or* by allowing another party to exploit those rights, such as licensing the audio rights to you.

TAKE-DOWN PROCEDURES: Federal law in the United States requires website owners to have procedures by which they can be notified of copyright infringing materials on their site, in order to have the material removed from the site. These procedures may vary from site to site, so search the site for their procedures and then follow that procedure to try to get your infringed materials off of someone else's page.

TERM: Term means how long your contract will be in effect.

WHOLESALER: A wholesaler is a company that buys from the publisher—notably you or through your distributor—and in turn sells the product to retailers. In the United States, an example of a wholesaler is Ingram Book Company in La Vergne, Tennessee.

WORK STOPPAGE: An action by a union admonishing its members not to work for a particular company unless and until they have fruitful negotiations.

Resources

BOOKS

The Untold History of the Talking Book by Matthew Rubery, published by Harvard University Press (2016)

BLOGGERS AND PODCASTS, in alphabetical order

- www.theaudiobookblog.com
- www.audiobookreviewer.com
- www.audiobookstoday.blogspot.com
- www.theaudiobookworm.com
- www.karencommins.com
- www.literatehousewife.com
- www.towerreview.com

COMPREHENSIVE LISTINGS

- www.audioeloquence.com is a compendium of sites specifically compiled to aid the audiobook industry.

COPYRIGHT SEARCH COMPANIES

- CompuMark: www.CompuMark.com

DICTIONARIES AND OTHER ONLINE ASSISTANCE: Many online dictionaries now have a little button to tap that will speak words aloud. I often use more than one dictionary to check whether they agree on a pronunciation. These include:

- Cambridge Dictionary (www.dictionary.cambridge.org)
- www.dictionary.com
- English Oxford *Living* Dictionaries (En.oxforddictionaries .com)
- www.merriam-webster.com

FORVO: Forvo is a wiki site, populated with pronunciations by people the world over. Recently it has come into vogue in the audiobook industry to discount the pronunciations precisely because it is a wiki, but I find it a valuable resource for authentic region-specific pronunciations, as well as pronunciation of words difficult to find elsewhere, such as scientific terms or Latin pronunciations. Something interesting about Forvo is that sometimes a word will not show up when you enter it in Arabic letters, but if you can find the native spelling of a word, such as in Chinese or Russian, it turns out the word actually is in the database.

GOOGLE: Sometimes I just type into a search engine "How to pronounce ..." along with the word I seek, and often that will guide me to a resource with the pronunciation.

GOOGLE TRANSLATE: Putting words into Google Translate will often bring up a pronunciation, as this resource has a speak function.

HOWJSAY: Howjsay is a site with a British narrator pronouncing many words. It is similar to a speaking dictionary. The site often provides both a U.S. and a U.K. pronunciation.

IPR: This website, iprlicense.com, lists rights available for sale. It is not comprehensive but if you are looking for rights without a specific title in mind, it might provide you with fodder. I have not used it.

LIBRARY OF CONGRESS: The Library of Congress has a site it calls Say How?, which spells out phonetic pronunciations of a large number of names. The URL is www.loc.gov/nls/about/organization/standards-guidelines/say-how/

MUSIC LIBRARIES: If you want to use music in a recording, music libraries tend to have a number of styles and lengths of clips you can license. There are many music libraries. Here are a few of them.

- De Wolfe Music at www.dewolfemusic.com
- Firstcom Music at www.firstcom.com
- Kool Kat at www.koolkat.sourceaudio.com/#!albums

NPR.ORG: NPR is another resource you can use to search for a name or word. Many of their articles have the transcript on the same page as the button for listening to the story, so you can look at the article to guess how far into the recording you need to go to find the pronunciation you seek.

PACKAGING AND CD REPLICATION

- Bowker issues ISBNs and bar codes for physical copies of your audiobooks. www.bowker.com/products/ISBN-US.html
- Disc Makers has a website at www.discmakers.com.
- Tri-Plex Packaging Corporation is a company that can handle both CD replication and packaging. They can be contacted by emailing Ken Golden at kgolden@tri-plexpkg.com or calling Tri-Plex Packaging Corporation at (646)747-5700.
- World Media Group is another manufacturer, with a website at www.worldmediagroup.com.

PIRACY MONITORING SERVICES: I have not used any of these providers and so cannot recommend any from my own experience but they are each used by some publishers.

- Covington & Burling, www.cov.com
- Digimarc (Attributor), www.digimarc.com
- Grayzone Services, www.grayzone.com
- Incopro, www.incoproip.com/
- Linkbusters, www.link-busters.com/
- MarkMonitor, www.markmonitor.com/
- NetNames, www.netnames.com/
- whiteBullet, www.white-bullet.com/

PRODUCTION HOUSES: A number of companies provide audiobook production services. If you choose to go this route, check their references and their pricing. Many of them are quite good. Here are a few, in alphabetical order:

- ACX: www.acx.com
- Author's Republic: www.authorsrepublic.com
- Deyan Audio Services, Inc.: www.deyanaudio.com (818)343-6131
- John Marshall Media: www.johnmarshallmedia.com (212)265-6066
- Findaway Voices: www.findawayvoices.com
- Lyric Audiobooks: www.lyricaudiobooks.com
- Mosaic Audio: www.mosaicaudio.com (818)268-3560

PUBLISHERSMARKETPLACE.COM: This is a publishing industry website and is invaluable for many reasons. You can peruse it as a nonmember, but paying for membership will grant you access to the full site. Many publishers and agents list book deals they have made, and that gives you an idea of what is coming up, and from whom. It also helps you to learn what types of books are published by various imprints or which agents represent which genres of books. This can aid you in your search for rights.

WIKIPEDIA: I list Wikipedia because it sometimes has the native language spelling of a word. Where it does, you can copy and paste it into Forvo or other pronunciation resources to see if that search brings up something you couldn't find previously.

YOUGLISH: YouGlish is a wonderful site. It has some of the same videos as YouTube, but rather than having to watch an entire video in hopes of hearing an elusive pronunciation, YouGlish will take you directly to the spot in the video where the word is said. It is a time-saver.

YOUTUBE: There are so many videos on YouTube that if you search for a specific name or word, you may find one or more videos with the pronunciation you seek. That said, these are often individuals who posted their own videos, so the pronunciations may be suspect.

Index